Library of
Davidson College

VOID

The Last Empire
Britain and the Commonwealth

The Last Empire
Britain and the Commonwealth

DAVID ADAMSON

I.B.TAURIS & Co Ltd
Publishers
London

Published by
I.B. Tauris & Co Ltd
110 Gloucester Avenue
London NW1 8JA

Copyright © 1989 by David Adamson

All rights reserved. Except for brief quotations in a review, this book, or any part thereof, must not be reproduced in any form without permission in writing from the Publisher.

British Library Cataloguing in Publication Data

Adamson, David
  The last empire : Britain and the Commonwealth.
  1. Commonwealth
  I. Title
  909'.09712410828

ISBN 1-85043-152-3

Printed and bound in Great Britain by
Biddles Ltd, Guildford and King's Lynn

Contents

	Acknowledgements	vii
	Introduction	1
1	Transition to the New Commonwealth	5
2	Ramphal's Secretariat	18
3	From Empire to Commonwealth	34
4	The South African matrix: ideals and magnanimity	46
5	Nassau: the first of a trilogy of troubled summits	61
6	Through Pretoria to Vancouver	73
7	The politics of aid	89
8	The international monarchy	104
9	The institutions: crumbling edifices, changing uses	119
10	The sporting Commonwealth	133
11	The mega-problems of mini-states	145
12	The Commonwealth and Britain	159
	Notes	177
	Index	189

Acknowledgements

I HAVE had a great deal of help in writing this book from a great many people who found time to talk to me. Some are mentioned in the chapter notes and text, but a considerable number are not, including some who have been the most helpful of all. My thanks to all of them, but especially to Patsy Robertson of the Commonwealth Secretariat, Prue Scarlett of the Commonwealth Trust/Royal Commonwealth Society (and the Trust's kindly librarians) and Dennis Austin of Manchester University.

Introduction

THE Commonwealth belongs in a special category of British institutions. It has its roots in our past, is visibly housed, it meets and debates, has inherited much affection and loyalty, and is in a state of decline which would be regarded as terminal if it were not for the fact that in British institutional life no one ever pulls the plug. The established Church and the House of Lords are lodged in the same category. Their purposes become increasingly difficult to define and justify, and at the same time inertia inhibits radical reform. Of course there are those who will instantly deny that the Commonwealth is British; it is a free-floating international organization of which Britain is merely a part. But that really is not true. It is not the English language or some sort of shared heritage which holds it together. What New Zealand, Sierra Leone and Belize have in common are their links with Britain. Without Britain the Commonwealth falls apart at once.

The Commonwealth is still in theory the third circle of British foreign policy, the bit of extra weight that makes Britain more than just the skilled middleman of the transatlantic world. Much has changed, though, since that theory was pronounced by Winston Churchill after the Second World War. The Commonwealth has ceased to be a military and economic alliance. A generation has grown up which no longer remembers when it did matter in that respect. What it may recall one day is that in the latter half of the 1980s the Commonwealth was stripped of what remained to it, its political pretensions. The 'sanctions summits' of 1985, 1986 and 1987 proved conclusively that it carries no entitlements when it comes to the formation of British policy. That is made increasingly in Europe, or in concert with the United States.

Mrs Thatcher's hand-bagging of the Commonwealth over sanctions against South Africa has passed into the folklore of her single-handed engagements with the rest of the world. What has not been generally noted has been the decline during the 1980s of the Commonwealth's institutions. The sizeable infrastructure bequeathed by the Empire or created specifically for the post-war Commonwealth has entered a phase of uncertainty and financial squeeze which is symbolized by the patches on the Commonwealth Institute's roof of Zambian copper. The parts of the infrastructure which are doing well are those which have broadened their horizons and internationalized themselves beyond the Commonwealth's boundaries.

The Old Commonwealth (namely, Britain, Canada, Australia and New Zealand) may have been at odds over sanctions, but they have been in agreement on the desirability of restraining the growth of the Commonwealth bureaucracy, even of cutting it back in some cases. In that respect it has been treated no differently from the agencies of the United Nations. Australia's Labour Government led the charge, demanding value for money and evidence of need. The 1988 bicentenary of Australia's foundation did not lead to a truce; in fact, it seems to have stimulated the fervour, mixing into it, according to some, an element of Pom-bashing resentment against the founders.

All this makes for hard times in the Commonwealth, an organization which, in its post-war manifestation, has rarely been blessed with really good times. Three things have come together at the end of the 1980s: the trauma of the sanctions summits, the need to appoint a new Secretary-General at the 1989 summit in Kuala Lumpur, and the approach of 1992, the 'Year of Europe', which will see Britain integrated more closely into the European Community despite Mrs Thatcher's resistance to even the faintest whiff of federalism. Together, they add up to the reason why this book is being written at this time.

The Commonwealth is a unique survivor, the relict of the liberalism which was always such a potent force in a remarkable empire. Whatever happens to it, it will not have a successor. It is very much the last empire. That implies an approaching end, but this book is not meant to be an epitaph. The Commonwealth has its enemies and a legion of sceptics, but the way ahead remains open for evolution and useful survival. I count myself among the sceptics, but an affectionate one.

At one of the Secretary-General's receptions which are a feature of the summits, an old friend in the Secretariat who knows my sometimes sour views took my arm and, turning me towards the assembly, said rebukingly, 'Look – this is the Commonwealth. Isn't it nice?' It is indeed nice, disarmingly so. It promotes causes and developments which are undeniably good. Its work in several areas is useful. But the sceptics' questions tend to centre on whether many of the promotions amount to much more than hot air blown in from tropical abodes of self-deception and self-promotion.

In a way, the Commonwealth is a victim of its decolonizing past. The ghost of Kwame Nkrumah still haunts its deliberations so far as many British Tories are concerned. They see its hallmarks as hypocrisy and bankrupt socialism of the sort more recently exemplified by Julius Nyerere's Tanzania. Others have not forgiven it for providing the emotional excuse which prevented Britain from committing itself to the European Community in the 1950s. From the other direction comes a torrid suspicion that Britain is run by racists whose actions are dictated by narrow self-interest.

Curiously, it is that same European Community which is blamed for Britain's retreat from the Commonwealth that now presents an opportunity for putting the organization on a new and more purposeful footing. The real value of the Commonwealth is not as a forum on racism but as a grouping which links a substantial part of the Third World through Britain and Canada to the industrial alliances which set the pace for the world economy. If there is to be a change of direction, it will depend on a British government which has often been dismissive of the Commonwealth giving a lead, not just to the Commonwealth, but to a British public whose opinions it has been adept at shaping. The Year of Europe could be the salvation of the Commonwealth, with Britain acting as its members' interlocutor and friend within the world's greatest trading community as it lowers its internal barriers and, inevitably, quickens the pace of its political as well as economic integration.

1
Transition to the New Commonwealth

ON THE north side of the Mall in London there is a reef of palaces and Nash terraces. The Commonwealth Secretariat is housed there in Marlborough House, a grace-and-favour palace whose interior an exiled godson of Louis XIV covered with paintings of Marlborough's great victory at Blenheim. Beyond its garden and trees, the theatre of the State enacts a daily spectacle, the plumes and scarlet uniforms the same as those of the soldiers who conquered or oversaw the acquisition of the Empire from which the post-war Commonwealth was born. Buckingham Palace and a suitably imposing memorial to Queen Victoria are at one end of the Mall; Admiralty Arch, symbol of the navy which guaranteed the integrity and security of the Empire, at the other. The Mall was completed only in 1913, a year before the war which saw the Empire reach its short-lived zenith of power and unity. On the Northern Indian plains, 6,000 miles away, Lutyens and Baker were, in the same year, drawing up their plans for the Raj's new capital at Delhi. But nothing is wasted in the ecocycle of Empire and its successors. A Sikh President sits in the salons which Lutyens designed for viceroys; he recognizes the Queen of England as Head of the Commonwealth to which republican India belongs; the Queen places Marlborough House, the home of Edward VII, Emperor of India, in his days as a wayward Prince of Wales, at the disposal of the Commonwealth Secretariat, whose current Secretary-General, Shridath Ramphal, is a Guyanese of Indian extraction.

Suitably housed in this hereditament of Empire and in cosy proximity to the monarch, the Commonwealth defies the finality of all the 'Farewells to Empire' which have been written and filmed. It even has a shrine nearby in Lancaster House, where, in the 1960s and 1970s, Britain surrendered its colonial empire in a rapid succession of independence conferences. Beyond the eastward end of the reef are the high commissions of the Old Commonwealth: New Zealand in a grey glass high-rise whose penthouse offers the best views in Central London; Canada House occupies the side of Trafalgar Square opposite to ex-Commonwealth member South Africa, whose embassy is permanently besieged by anti-apartheid demonstrators beating bongo drums and chanting slogans through loudhailers; and, finally, near the end of the Strand, there is Australia House.

One other important element has to be placed in this scene: Downing Street, with No. 10 on one side and the Foreign and Commonwealth Office on the other. Between the former imperial masters and the Secretariat on the far side of St James's Park exists what might politely be called an adversarial relationship. It differs markedly from the relationship between Buckingham Palace and the Secretariat. The Queen loves the Commonwealth, New and Old; it is what makes her the world's only international monarch. Under the formula agreed when India was allowed into the Commonwealth in 1949/50 as a republic, she is Head of the Commonwealth, a title which is ceremonial and symbolic and in no way constitutional. Of the Commonwealth's present 48 members, she is Queen of 17.

The Commonwealth's role as one of the three interlocking circles of policy which Winston Churchill saw as the means of maintaining British influence in the age of superpowers remains part of Whitehall's official dogma. There is Europe as one circle; the special relationship with the United States as another; and then, finally, the Commonwealth. Even in the 1940s and 1950s the Commonwealth – and the world – was changing too fast for the third circle to be entirely convincing. Today, it would be plain unrealistic to think of it as a basis for policy-making. It exists in the dogma largely because removing it would cause diplomatic upset. So the Commonwealth ring exists rather shadowily, like the remains of a neolithic encampment revealed by aerial photography. It shows up more strongly only when an oblique light is cast on it, as, for example, when Mrs Thatcher denounces the vision of a politically federated Europe and, by implication, demonstrates that the instincts of British governments remain true to the wider world beyond the ocean.

Most histories of the Commonwealth and its evolution give 1949 as the year in which the New Commonwealth was born. The formula under which Pandit Nehru accepted King George VI as 'the symbol of the free association of its [the Commonwealth's] independent member nations'[1] represented a long step back from previous British positions which had made allegiance to the King the *sine qua non* of Commonwealth membership. When Prime Minister, Clement Attlee had tried to soften the question of sovereignty, something which Nehru found quite impossible to accommodate within the draft Indian constitution. As he wrote to Nehru on 20 March 1949:[2]

The Crown is an abstract symbol connoting authority, often connected in the minds of some with an external power, But the real link is a person, The King. At the head of the Commonwealth is a family. The family does in a very real sense symbolise the family nature of the Commonwealth.... We are fortunate in having a Royal Family that does inspire affection not only among those who know them but among millions who have not seen them in person. People see in the Royal Family a projection of the family life which they hold dear.

Who better to understand that than Nehru, second in line of a dynasty that has stretched so far from his father, Motilal, through his daughter, Indira, to his grandson, Rajiv. The 'Head of the Commonwealth' formula emerged and was accepted and Nehru explained it to the Constituent Assembly in lukewarm terms. It was 'beneficial' to all parties concerned. 'It is better to keep a co-operative association going which may do good in this world rather than break it.'[3]

The Australian Prime Minister, Robert Menzies, an old-fashioned King's Man and the last who could be called an

Imperial Statesman, saw the change as not so much the birth
of the New Commonwealth (for which he had no enthusiasm, even though he learned to live with it) as the end of the old one, with its close ties of blood, tradition and personal friendships and loyalties, the latter fire-hardened in two wars. 'Britain is at war, therefore Australia is at war', he had announced to the Australian people, without consulting his parliament, on the outbreak of the Second World War. The terms of India's membership meant that at one stroke allegiance to the Crown had ceased to be the bond of union. Menzies wrote in his autobiography:[4]

It would, I think, be unduly naive to imagine that the phrase 'The Head of the Commonwealth' can be expected to mean very much to the private citizens of republics. As years go on, it will mean less and less, until in due course it may evoke no more response than would be evoked by an acknowledgement that 'X' is recognised as President of the General Assembly of the United Nations.

Menzies had an adoring attitude towards the monarchy that nowadays one would associate with tabloid readers rather than with a prime minister. He was out of office and in London with his wife and daughter in November 1948 when Prince Charles was born and his account of mingling with the crowds outside Buckingham Palace indicates the robust simplicity of his affection for the royal family.

At such an event he thought one could begin to understand the place of the British Crown in the hearts and minds of those who held allegiance to it. The cheers and goodwill of the crowd calling for the royal family to appear on the Palace balcony were those of a democracy which saw the Crown not as its opponent but as its focal point. It is hard to imagine Bob Hawke, the current Australian Prime Minister, who believes the monarchy will be ended in Australia by the end of the century,[5] standing at the Palace gates and cheering, or any other Old Commonwealth prime minister, for that matter. Certainly not Mrs Thatcher, who has a somewhat distant relationship with the monarch. Times were changing fast when Menzies wrote his book in the 1960s, and he took a gloomy view of the future of the Commonwealth. As he had watched the New Commonwealth develop and listened to 'the language of attack', he had become increasingly conscious of danger. If it turned out that the New Commonwealth had been called into existence to break up the basic unity of the old, we might end up with no Commonwealth at all, and that, in his view, would be a 'world tragedy'.

In early 1962, at the time of Britain's first, and unsuccessful, attempt to join the European Community (vetoed by de Gaulle on the grounds that Britain was not 'European' in its attitudes and carried too much Commonwealth and American baggage), the views of the then Secretary for Commonwealth Relations, Duncan Sandys, were published in a pamphlet – *The Modern Commonwealth* – put out by his ministry. He had made it a practice, he wrote, to keep other Commonwealth countries in touch with developments which Britain thought of international importance to all of them, such as nuclear tests, Laos, the Congo and Berlin. There was a reciprocal flow of information from Britain's Commonwealth partners.

From time to time it has been suggested that a joint 'Commonwealth secretariat' should be set up. It is argued that this would strengthen the links between us. But the proposal has so far been resisted on the grounds that a new organisation of this kind would inevitably cut across the direct personal relations between ministers and officials in different Commonwealth countries, which is such a special feature of our association.

Did the New Commonwealth really begin with India's accession, or should one start with the creation of the Secretariat in 1965? Had it really been such a radical step to demote the monarchy? The 'direct personal relations' between the leaders and between their officials were surely more basic to the spirit of the Commonwealth than the monarch, however, important he or she might be as a symbol of unity. After all, assuming that the Attlee government was firmly committed to a multi-racial Commonwealth which included the dependent colonies, it can hardly have expected that the liberalizing tide would bring with it universal acceptance among the liberated that they should become monarchical democracies. Such a dilution of sovereignty in young states striving to build a sense of nationhood was never very likely, although perhaps even at that time no one foresaw the speed with which the new, preponderantly republican, Commonwealth would be created, with even the smallest and most backward colonies rushed into independence. The last Commonwealth prime ministers' summit attended by Menzies, in London, in June 1965, saw the approval of the Agreed Memorandum which established the Secretariat, and removed central control of Commonwealth affairs from Britain. In effect it institutionalized Southern Africa as the central issue at the summits. The Crown was no longer an issue, but race was. And since it was specifically race in Southern Africa which was the issue, it meant that the British government was more or less permanently in the dock at summits organized by an independent secretariat whose positions, as voiced by the Secretary-General, inevitably reflected the fact that the New Commonwealth was largely a Third World organization. It had become a little too like the United Nations for British tastes.

The African dimension

The ferment which brought about the change came from the new African members. When Ghana became a member – the first in black Africa – in 1957 under Kwame Nkrumah, a marxist whose impulses wrecked the economy and ended democracy, South Africa was a member of the Commonwealth and Roy Welensky was Prime Minister of a Central African Federation incorporating the territories which were later to become Zambia, Malawi and Zimbabwe. Ghana was followed by Nigeria in 1960, Sierra Leone and Tanganyika (since 1964 Tanzania) in 1961, Uganda in 1962, Kenya in 1963, and Malawi and Zambia in 1964. Of the 19 members of the Commonwealth in 1964, eight were African. Joe Garner, Permanent Under-Secretary in the Commonwealth Office at the time, called it 'the African dimension', and it filled him with dismay since its consequences led inexorably through the creation of the Secretariat to the absorption of the Commonwealth Office into the Foreign Office.[6]

The place of Asia as the continent of dynamic change in the fifties was seized in the sixties by the stridency of Africa. After the independence explosion of the 1960s, the African nations provided a striking example of a pressure group exploiting to the full the techniques of propaganda available to international diplomacy. These efforts perhaps drew additional strength and bitterness from the domestic campaign being carried on at the same time by the Blacks within the USA.

It was the spirit of the times, of course, and African dictators carried greater weight in liberal and left-wing circles (and were more obsessively attacked by the right wing) than they do today. The civil rights campaign in the United States lent moral force to African demands, and no one was better placed to act as a prism for the crusading influences than Nkrumah, educated by Lincoln and Pennsylvania Universities in the United States; President of the African Students Organization of America and Canada; a law student in London, where he registered but did not take his Doctorate in Philosophy; and a ready-made convert to the ideas of W. E. B. Dubois, the American father of Pan-Africanism, and Marcus Garvey, the Jamaican who preached that the only way in which blacks would find their salvation would be through a free and independent Africa.

South Africa left the Commonwealth in 1961, mourned by a depressed Harold Macmillan, the British Prime Minister of the time, although in retrospect it is hard to see why he, or Menzies, could ever have believed that its racial policies would be compatible with remaining in the Old Commonwealth, let alone the new one. Garner found that life at the Commonwealth Office was like being in a film which had been speeded up to 'a ridiculous rate where everything happens at once and the characters seem to be rushing in all directions'. In this Harold Lloyd scenario crisis followed crisis unpredictably, problems arose everywhere and the double standard prevailed, to the mounting indignation of Menzies. The criteria for independence were lowered and (wrote Garner) 'any territory however small, impoverished and defenceless received independence, and later the mini-states, with recognition as members of the United Nations, gained acceptance on the world stage and could scarcely be denied Commonwealth status'.[7] Intimacy disappeared from the once club-like atmosphere of the summits, as did discussion, constructive or otherwise, about matters other than Southern Africa. Sir Alec Douglas-Home, when Prime Minister in 1964, put together a package of proposals on Commonwealth cooperation, but found it submerged by African insistence on using the summit to discuss Rhodesia. The meeting took on the acrimonious character of a session of the UN General Assembly.

The Secretariat

Under the old, previously unchallenged, convention, it had always been the British Cabinet Secretary who acted as secretary-general to the Commonwealth conferences, but, according to Garner, by 1964 his position had become 'intolerable'. He could no longer operate in the 'gentlemanly tradition' of the British civil service and at the same time counter the attacks made on him, his handling of the conference and the policies of his government. Nkrumah, in a burst of Commonwealth enthusiasm, tabled the idea of a secretariat to handle the organization's affairs, a short-lived and final burst, as it happened. He pulled Ghana out of the Commonwealth following Rhodesia's UDI in November 1965 and was overthrown by a coup in the following year.

The British accepted the Secretariat in a mood combining fatalism and exhaustion. It was an old idea which had been kicking its heels in the wings since the first years of the century when imperial federation enjoyed a vogue. Despite Duncan Sandys' earlier hostility to the idea, he had raised it – he was Commonwealth Secretary at the time – in talks earlier in 1964 with Lester Pearson, the Canadian Prime Minister, who backed away from earlier objections (traditionally the Canadians had feared that any Commonwealth machinery would be 'Downing Street machinery'). Canadian agreement was given at the 1965 summit; Pearson's Cabinet sent him a message saying that it was an unwelcome development with which they concurred solely on the grounds that Canada should avoid adopting a negative posture.[8] The other important Old Commonwealth country, Australia, wanted the Secretary-General to keep a low profile and did not like the idea of his being ranked equal with a senior high commissioner. But Britain's position as the Commonwealth's director had become untenable and it was accepted that if the organization was to survive there had to be a change. 'The idea of a multinational secretariat was no doubt regarded as in the interests of some of the new members' wrote Garner. 'It was no less emphatically in British interests.'[9]

The Conservatives lost the October 1964 election and Harold Wilson's Labour government came to power. Cledwyn Hughes (now Lord Cledwyn) was Minister of State for Commonwealth Relations in the new government. He revealed in a recent interview:[10]

Joe Garner didn't like the Secretariat, but he accepted it. What he was violently against was the merger of the Commonwealth Office with the Foreign Office [which took place in 1968]... He realized that the Commonwealth Office would be the junior partner. And there was also the fact that the Commonwealth trained diplomat was a different creature from the Foreign Office diplomat. The Commonwealth man regarded his responsibilities as a family matter. He was looked upon in the countries concerned as friend, mentor, and guide.

Which could be translated as meaning that he was not such a hard-nosed professional as his colleagues, a bit of a soft touch perhaps when sentiment and history were called into play. A vestigial remnant of the old Commonwealth Office remains within today's Foreign and Commonwealth Office in the shape of a small Commonwealth Co-ordination Department, and heads of mission in Commonwealth countries are designated as high commissioners instead of as ambassadors, but the career structure makes no distinction between the 'family' and the rest of the world.

The Agreed Memorandum on the Secretariat approved at the June 1965 summit laid down a suitably uncontroversial and non-meddlesome role for the Secretary-General, with several points underscored for the benefit of the Africans and any others who had not fully grasped the essentially bromidic nature of the club rules.

The Secretary-General and his staff should approach their task bearing in mind that the Commonwealth is an association which enables countries in different regions of the world, consisting of a variety of races and representing a number of interests and points of view, to exchange opinions in a friendly, informal and intimate atmosphere.

It was not a formal organization and it did not encroach on the sovereignty of its members. Nor did it try to reach collective decisions or take united action. Consultation was its life blood. At the same time, the Memorandum has in places a point-counter-point quality which indicates a drafting committee not entirely of one mind: the Secretariat should not arrogate to itself executive functions; the Secretariat should have a constructive role. The Secretariat should disseminate factual information; factual information cannot be precisely defined. Provided the Secretary-General proceeded with circumspection, he was authorized to prepare and circulate papers on international questions of common concern, but these papers must not 'propagate any particular sectional or partisan points of view, [must] contain no policy judgments or recommendations by the Secretariat and [must] not touch upon the internal affairs of a member country or disputes or serious differences between two or more member countries'. Accordingly, the Secretariat was urged to begin modestly, to be guided by the principles laid down and to be careful not to trespass on the independence and sovereignty of the members 'whose servant it will be'. If it obeyed those injunctions it would be possible for it to grow in the spirit of the Commonwealth association and develop as a unifying element.

The Commonwealth has had two Secretary-Generals and both have interpreted the Memorandum as being fairly elastic in its constraints. One man's elasticity is another's excessive licence and suspicion and disagreement have fretted the relationship between the Secretariat and the British government. The first Secretary-General, Arnold Smith, a distinguished Canadian diplomat whose career ranged from editing *The Baltic Times* in pre-war Estonia to being Canadian ambassador to the Soviet Union, believed his office was bugged by MI5; he took visitors for a walk in the Marlborough House garden when he wished to talk confidentially.[11] His experiences in Moscow enabled him, he claimed, to detect small signs indicating that the telephones in his flat and his office – magnificently situated in Queen Mary's old bedroom – were being tapped. A more definite sign of not being entirely popular was the Commonwealth Office's desire to prevent him from getting ideas above what they considered to be his station. Its handouts referred to him not as Commonwealth Secretary-General but as 'Secretary-General of the Commonwealth Secretariat', a subtly limiting title. Smith's feeling of persecution was inflamed further when the Secretariat's staff were moved out of the main part of Marlborough House into the servants' quarters, a move which he saw as an attempt to diminish their status. He was to receive another affront at his first finance ministers' meeting that same year when he found that the British had advised the Jamaican organizers that he should be seated separately at a small table at the centre of the horseshoe conference table, 'like a UN stenographer'. He defeated that move by arranging with the Jamaicans to be placed next to the chairman. There was another victory when Prince Philip noticed that Smith and his wife had been placed at the end of a line of *chargés d'affaires* attending a Buckingham Palace reception. The Prince inquired why they occupied such a humble position and then remarked that it was the Commonwealth Office which arranged such things. Thereafter Smith was placed with the Papal representative and ahead of the ambassadors.

During Smith's ten years in the Secretariat there was what he has described as 'a shift in the nature and working of the Commonwealth from residual but significant Anglocentricity to full multilateralism'. They were years in which emotion was at its flood over white Rhodesia's UDI and Smith saw his task as that of preventing a British 'sell-out' on terms unacceptable to the rest of the Commonwealth. 'Interference' by the Commonwealth Secretariat in Britain's handling of what it considered a matter for the British alone was always a sensitive issue and successive governments made strenuous efforts to keep ahead of the game through human and electronic intelligence gathering. Smith's suspicions about his telephones may well have been justified.

Smith's memoirs have a foreword fulsome in its praise for Britain ('A hundred years from now, I suggest, historians will consider the Commonwealth the greatest of all Britain's contributions to man's social and political history'), but the tone of much of the rest of the book suggests that he felt he was dealing with British politicians who lacked both backbone and a long view of events. On the prime Rhodesian issue commitments had to be 'extracted' or 'won'; the Commonwealth made it 'virtually impossible' for Britain to conclude a settlement with the white minority regime; Harold Wilson was a tactician not a strategist; unlike the governments of Wilson and Heath, the other Commonwealth governments kept a strategic objective in view, majority rule. Above all, the issue became a race between Britain concluding a settlement with Ian Smith and Britain recognizing the growing economic strength of Nigeria. 'As the British gradually recognised that the financial see-saw was tipping towards independent Africa, the danger of a sell-out receded.'

Nigeria's post-independence record includes a series of military governments and a civil war fought on racial lines, which would hardly entitle it to moral leadership of the sort Smith suggests. The whites who declared Rhodesia independent may have been selfish, short-sighted and racist, but the rights and wrongs of the situation, and the best way to proceed, were never exactly crystal clear, any more than they are today in South Africa. No British political party supported the Rhodesian whites, but that was not a reflection of enthusiasm among the electorate for the black cause. The imposition of UN mandatory sanctions was as far as any British government would, or dared, go. African rights were not seen in Britain as a cause worth fighting for, even though the Rhodesian whites behaved unjustly. The popular image of black Africa was an unsavoury composite of intolerance and incompetence, of one-party states and double standards.

Outside the political cadres of the Left and middle-class liberal circles, there was scant sympathy for or understanding of the problems of black leaders, often good and genuinely kindly men, but equally men of limited experience and raw sensitivities.

In his *Survey of Commonwealth Affairs 1953–69*, Professor Bruce Miller, an Australian, quotes an unnamed British official on what he saw as the psychological reasons for African hyperbole in their early confrontations with the British.[12]

The Africans are by nature aggressive and self-assertive, condemned by history to be inexperienced, in outlook simplistic and idealistic; ambitious but unsure of themselves and on the defensive; emotional and apt to be bitter; their inferiority complex is easily aroused and they readily see the rest of the world banded against them as it was in the last century.

British views have not changed much, if at all, since then. And no doubt the British are still as maddeningly evasive and diplomatically reassuring.

2
Ramphal's Secretariat

THERE IS a convention, fuzzily defined, within the Commonwealth that each region should take its turn in choosing a Secretary-General. Arnold Smith came from the founder-member of the Old Commonwealth, Canada. It might have been expected that his successor would come from India, the oldest member of the New Commonwealth, but the choice went to the Caribbean. Shridath Ramphal, Foreign Minister of Guyana and of Asian origin, was duly appointed (after receiving an affirmatory stamp of approval from Mrs Gandhi) by the heads of government at their 1975 meeting in Kingston, Jamaica. His term of office was extended in 1980 and again in the mid-1980s. It ends in mid-1990 and 'Sonny' (as he is widely and familiarly known) says he will not stand again (not that everyone believes him).

It has been a long reign, perhaps a disappointingly long one for him, since the Secretary-Generalship of the Commonwealth has not turned out to be a stepping-stone to the Secretary-Generalship of the United Nations. Despite denials at the time, he lobbied hard for that job in 1981, but it went to Perez de Cuellar, a sober-sided Peruvian diplomat. The UN likes gravitas in its secretary-generals. It may be a misleading quality, as Perez de Cuellar's predecessor Kurt Waldheim has proved, but it is a necessary one and one with which Sonny is not over-endowed. However, even if he had taken on board enough to sink the UN building beneath the East River, his chances of success would have been very slim. Lord Carrington, the British Foreign Secretary at the time, had let it be known that he would gladly swim the Atlantic to stop Sonny. Britain is one of the five permanent members of the Security Council, an influential state when it comes to moulding the contours of the UN, and easily capable of stopping in its tracks any Third World band-wagon which the Commonwealth Secretary-General might have been trying to line up. The Americans said 'no' too, and the Russians told Ramphal he reminded them of their bête noir Hammarskjold. 'I suppose that what I knew, but didn't want to admit, was that the major powers, in particular the superpowers, do not want an effective United Nations', Ramphal explained two years later, evidently still chagrined by the experience.[1]

The Commonwealth was not exactly a dynamic organization even in 1975 and it is hard to imagine that Ramphal ever saw it as the summit of his career. By any standards he was a successful man. He had read law at London University and been called to the Bar from Gray's Inn. He had worked on the ill-fated attempt to create a West Indian Federation, and when that collapsed went to Harvard Law School for a year on a Guggenheim Fellowship. He drafted Guyana's independence constitution, became its Attorney-General and, in the early 1970s, held the portfolios of Foreign Affairs and Justice. The Queen knighted him in 1970, when he was 42, her advisers having decided they had spotted a winner. He has never used the title and tries to discourage the press and others from using it; a plain 'Mr' sits better with Sonny's Third World egalitarianism. 'As Secretary-General', says the potted biography put out by the Secretariat, 'Mr Ramphal has seen it as his vocation to be an advocate for the dispossessed and to highlight the imperatives of a less unequal society on which Commonwealth leaders have been outspoken.'

Ramphal was surprised by the number of people who tried to discourage him from taking the Commonwealth Secretary-Generalship:[2]

So many said to me 'Are you sure? Isn't this thing on the way out? Shouldn't you be looking more to the UN, to the Third World, to the non-aligned rather than to a dying institution?' I mean, it wasn't all as crude as that, but that was the kind of nuances I got from quite a lot of people.

He asked Indira Gandhi what she thought and she said much the same as the others.

And I said then, 'Well, I have thought a lot about it in the light of comments from people and I don't think it's a dying institution, or certainly I don't think it needs to be. I think it's the kind of institution the world badly needs, because it is the only thing outside the UN which really crosses the divides.' She thought about it a little bit and she said 'If you feel you can do something about it, do. But make sure you give it a good push into the end years of the century.' So she was encouraging me in the end to take it on, but saying that if I did, I should see it in a dynamic way.

Sonny is a likeable man. He is amiable, helpful and there is absolutely no side to him. He means what he says in his reedy West Indian lilt about race and South Africa and is not deflected by awareness of the emotions ranging from hostility to irritation aroused in Old Commonwealth breasts by his unrelenting use of the Secretariat to consolidate pressure against Pretoria. 'Stick to taking the minutes', the former New Zealand Premier Sir Robert Muldoon advised him publicly at the 1981 Melbourne summit in the course of a row over whether the All Blacks should play the Springboks. But to no avail. It was not naiveté which had got him into a constant scrape over apartheid, noted an Old Commonwealth diplomat, adding wryly that he had the best tuned political antennae in the business. Has his calculated grandstanding on the north bank of the Limpopo really done much to breach apartheid, however, or has it merely revealed, to its detriment, the inherent unfitness of the Commonwealth for service in the front line? Expectations have been raised, left unfulfilled and disillusionment has set in. On the other hand, no African country has left the Commonwealth in protest against the meagre results of the last three summits. And for that at least, Ramphal deserves credit, even if the self-interest of the Africans is the biggest reason for their staying put. He has both strained the Commonwealth's structure and kept it together. The biennial row over South Africa is, after all, for some of the members what the Commonwealth is all about – a chance to vent their frustrations.

Relations with the British Government

Ramphal speaks with damped-down bitterness about the British Government's attitude during the 1979–80 Rhodesian settlement which produced Zimbabwe. Carrington's distrust of him, so evident during the Lancaster House constitutional conference, is believed by some to have come from reading transcripts of his monitored conversations with the leaders of the Patriotic Front of Joshua Nkomo and Robert Mugabe (which he thought should win the ensuing election and which the British hoped would lose). Certainly, Ramphal has come to a fairly philosophical endorsement of Arnold Smith's belief that MI5 is prepared to bug the Secretary-General's office. The Secretariat was refused observer status during the conference ('Lock the doors! It's that bugger Ramphal trying to get in', Carrington is reported to have said with jocular ferocity when the security men reported that somebody was prowling around outside) and Ramphal was told firmly by the Foreign Office that he would not be welcome in Rhodesia-Zimbabwe before or during the elections.

We take a big part of the credit for Lusaka [the 1979 summit at which the draft document for negotiations was agreed]. The British government has constantly and consistently refused to admit that this had anything to do with the Commonwealth. That it was Mrs Thatcher and Peter Carrington and all that. Well, we know differently. They say Mrs Thatcher went to Lusaka with everything in her handbag, but I drafted the ten points! In a sense, though, I don't have a big fight over that. It is part of a Secretary's role to allow governments to take credit for things you have nudged them into. That's all right. We are not seeking glory. What I think is not fair is when a government which has been encouraged to move in that direction, and does so, turns round and beats the Secretary on the back.[3]

He thought the Secretariat was refused observer status at Lancaster House because Ian Smith, the Rhodesian Prime

Minister, would have objected, and also because Carrington wanted as total a control of the process and its subsequent stages as he could get. 'He saw me and the Secretariat as a variable quantity he could not absolutely control, and so better we were out.' Later, however, Carrington was obliged to concede an observer role to the Commonwealth during the elections, on the insistence of the Patriotic Front.

Carrington's version of events portrays the Commonwealth as a basically hostile forum which had to be manipulated and generally kept in its place. In his memoirs he dismisses with a caustic 'nonsense' the idea that Lancaster House was attributable to a Commonwealth initiative in which Britain reluctantly concurred.[4]

Margaret Thatcher and I arrived at Lusaka with perfectly clear intentions of what we wanted to achieve. We knew what we wanted and we got it. Margaret played the hand extremely well, and bore with equanimity a certain amount of predictable abuse from some of her Commonwealth colleagues, delivered at banquets as well as at meetings.

What Ramphal sees as his desire to be helpful during the conference is downgraded by Carrington to something less obliging.

As ever, the most trying occasions generally took place out of the conference room itself. I remember having to keep Sonny Ramphal ... from interfering. Having been present at the Lusaka conference he thought, no doubt with the best of intentions, that he could help and had the right to try. He was mistaken, and I spent some time persuading him of the fact: totally committed to the Patriotic Front, he had no credibility as an impartial observer.

Distrust between the government and the Secretariat flourished in a rich soil in the first year of Mrs Thatcher's administration and moved rapidly from the Rhodesian issue to its successor, South Africa. Ramphal is too deeply engaged in the latter campaign to admit to any discouragement caused by Thatcher's refusal to adopt comprehensive sanctions. 'We have got quite far without Britain', he says.

The Commonwealth's disputes over South Africa only flare up at the summits, when they hit the headlines for a few days. In the long intervals between, the Commonwealth rarely makes news. It is not for want of trying. Ramphal's speeches, put out by *Commonwealth Information*, have eye-catching headlines such as 'Rage, Rage Against the Dying of the Light' and 'Why the Bell of Apartheid Tolls for Everyone'. There are no half-measures. The death of Mozambique's President Machel in an air crash on South African territory is firmly attributed to South African destabilization. The brutal methods applied by Pretoria to black children are described as 'the most savage and inhuman treatment meted out to the young by any state power since biblical times', which even as it puts P. W. Botha on a par with King Herod seems to let Adolf Hitler and the Khmer Rouge off the hook. Mrs Thatcher gets short shrift:[5]

Resistance to sanctions lies in the cold unfeeling calculus of money and profit and returns. And it is bolstered here and there by the self-deception (unarticulated for the most part) that white 'kith and kin' could not really be guilty of such atrocities; that South African society is inherently decent and that if matters are out of hand occasionally, they cannot be substantially to blame. This stubborn sympathy defies the facts and it comes, too, from countries who, by having enjoyed lengthy social and economic ties with South Africa, are the very economies who have benefited most from the economic deprivations inherent in the apartheid system.

Behind passages such as this and much of the other rhetoric there is an evident doubt in Ramphal's mind (and not his alone, it should be said) about whether the Thatcher government really 'cares' about the Commonwealth. Is it really committed? He told the Royal Commonwealth Society in 1981:

I know how deeply the Queen as Head of the Commonwealth cares about the Commonwealth, how positive is Her Majesty's role in personifying as Head of the Commonwealth the association's highest aspirations, its reach across many differences to common values – and high among them a sense of caring for each other and for the

Commonwealth. But how often do I not worry whether in the great machine of government beats there a Commonwealth heart; whether in the domain of policy stirs a spirit of belonging? For how many does the Commonwealth seem to be 'the others' – as if the others 'overseas' had collectively become the Commonwealth and Britain was somehow, and somewhat surprisingly, associated with it – but was not of it?

Ramphal has said more recently (to the author) that he believes Britain's acknowledgement of the importance of the Commonwealth will return, but he hopes it will not take too long. He points to the education of Commonwealth students in Britain (where substantial cuts in financial assistance have been made) as the area where he feels the most damage is being done. 'Take the case of Botswana. The government there awards ten scholarships a year. This year (1988) it had to place them all outside Britain because it couldn't afford to send them here.'

The image of an 'uncaring' Britain is a perception which has obviously occurred to Mrs Thatcher and her post-1983 Foreign and Commonwealth Secretary, Sir Geoffrey Howe. Following the débâcles of the last three summits, in Nassau, London and Vancouver, there was evidence in a few small signs early in 1988 that the government had decided the time had come for fence-mending. Mrs Thatcher turned up unexpectedly at the Commonwealth Day service in Westminster Abbey in March; for the first time in recent memory the Foreign Office issued a Commonwealth Day statement, in the Foreign Secretary's name, declaring that 'Britain remains firmly committed to the Commonwealth'; and the BBC's World Service (which is financed out of the Foreign Office budget) let it be known that it planned to broadcast the Commonwealth Day service in 1989. By the late autumn of 1988, though, the mood seemed once again to have become 'uncaring'. The Secretariat noted a singular omission from the Queen's Speech at the State Opening of Parliament, a statement of the government's programme and policy for the ensuing year: there was no mention of the Commonwealth. That had not happened before during the more than two decades of the Secretariat's existence.

In the British Government's eyes, of course, the Secretariat and the Commonwealth are not synonymous. The Commonwealth is heritage; the Secretariat is the encumbrance that has to be accepted, a sort of National Trust that has enabled Britain to enjoy the stately home bequeathed it by valiant and sagacious ancestors, even if, regrettably, it has had to be opened to so many intrusive and undesirable influences. The Commonwealth is not just about summits and ministerial meetings organized by the Secretariat. It is about 'contacts at every level, between many different groups, organisations and individuals', according to a FCO statement of 14 March 1988.

Finance and organization

Similarly, of course, the Secretariat is not just about Southern Africa. It is about quite a number of things, perhaps too many things, and its organization, the ordering of priorities and the funding of the Secretariat's and other Commonwealth budgets have been under scrutiny by the major contributors since the 1987 Vancouver summit. Some countries have not paid their shares of the budget and there have been demands for a review of the scale of contributions. It is no use poor countries demanding so many programmes if they are not prepared to help fund them, is the complaint of the rich. Other complaints focus on the unwillingness of Secretariat officials to make decisions. 'Things tend to freeze up', said an Old Commonwealth diplomat. 'Every decision has to be made by the Secretary-General.'

Two very large rent increases in 1987 and 1988 confronted the Secretariat with the realities of what it costs to have offices in Central London. For years the British government charged a peppercorn rent for No. 10 Carlton House Terrace, once the town house of Mr Gladstone and now the offices of the Secretariat's economic section. 'Suddenly', says Ramphal, 'it was all market forces.' The Secretariat was obliged to pay a rent of £230,000. Then there was the problem caused by the fact that when central heating was installed in Marlborough House many decades ago the contractor failed to realize that the unaccustomed heat would shrink its ancient timbers. Structural changes added to the problems. Repairing the damage has been a slow process and has meant gradually moving the staff elsewhere. Ramphal and his senior staff moved into No. 2 Carlton Gardens, in back-to-back proximity to the Foreign Secretary's official residence. But most of the staff went to Quadrant House on the other side of Pall Mall, facing Marlborough House, where the rent in 1988 was £1,020,000 a year. The Secretariat in that year was accommodated in six separate buildings and paying a total in rents, rates, and general overheads of £1,868,000 out of its annual budget.

The Secretariat's complaint that it was being thrown to the mercies of the London property market received an unsympathetic hearing from the Foreign Office, which riposted with a claim that the government was spending £11m. on the repair and restoration of Marlborough House. The Secretariat had been given Marlborough House rent-free under the 1965 Memorandum and it was not the British Government's responsibility if it had grown so large that it required additional accommodation. It had the option of cutting its staff to numbers that would fit into Marlborough House when the repairs were completed; or it could seek a second office in one of the cheaper parts of London or its surroundings. An option for which the Foreign Office lobbied hard among Commonwealth countries was the idea of moving all except a handful of senior officials to a new office outside London; Oxford, Cambridge and Hemel Hempstead were among the places mentioned. The scene was further complicated by Prince Charles's desire to return to Marlborough House, the traditional home of the Prince of Wales (see Chapter 8 on the monarchy for a fuller account).

At £6.5m. the Secretariat's budget is considerably less than, for example, the amount Britain is giving Tanzania to improve its dry cargo facilities. Britain pays 30 per cent of the budget, Canada 16 per cent, Australia 8 per cent and the rest is shared out among the other members. Symptomatic of the Secretariat's current standing is the agreement among the Old Commonwealth countries that it should be regarded in the same way as the UN's agencies and held to zero-growth.

The struggle over its finances and accommodation spilled over to a meeting of senior officials in the Seychelles in November 1988 when New Commonwealth countries rallied to its support and accused Britain of failing in its responsibility as the host country. An inconclusive argument led to a decision to set up a committee composed of high commissioners and a British government representative to look into the problem.

If the Secretariat got more money it would simply waste it, was the blunt opinion of a Commonwealth diplomat. There was a lack of accounting and there was 'this blob of bureaucracy'. Keeping it on a tight rein helped focus its collective mind. Criticisms which recur in Old Commonwealth circles are that there are too many people in junior positions, too much overtime, too much travel, too many posts occupied on a 'jobs for Third World boys' basis (allocation is a tricky business, as it is with the UN; 30 of the 48 member states are represented on the Secretariat's staff).

At the beginning of 1988 Manchester University's Emeritus Professor of Government, Dennis Austin, a man of wide experience in Commonwealth matters, observed in a Chatham House paper[6] that the Secretariat had multiplied its functions without greatly strengthening its position. He added that Ramphal had enlarged the office since the days of his predecessor, Arnold Smith, and quoted his justification that it was 'a necessary growth, necessary both to dissolve the residual film of Anglo-centricity that was distorting its image and to support its increasingly functional dynamism'.[7] Ramphal was sufficiently stung by the implied criticism of unjustified enlargement that he ordered his staff to produce a comparison of the figures. He told the author in mid-1988:[8]

It's something like an increase of 22 in 13 years. There is a feeling that the Commonwealth is doing a lot more, so it must be bigger. The CFTC [Commonwealth Fund for Technical Co-operation] has grown a bit more. It was just beginning when I came, with a budget of £5m, and it is now up to about £25m. I was really clear in my mind that I wasn't coming to make the thing a big bureaucracy. I wanted it to be more intellectual. I wanted it to do more in the area of ideas. And I suppose that I would hope that if there is one thing that is a valid claim, it is that while it hasn't grown as a bureaucracy, it has deepened as a think tank and a catalyst.

It is not immediately easy to think of areas where the Secretariat has acted as a think-tank in the manner of, say, Chatham House, and, in fact, the idea of creating one was rather knocked on the head at a recent conference.[9] Think-tanks need receptive audiences in governments and politics if they are to be effective, and would the Commonwealth be able to find them? it was asked pertinently by someone who runs one. In the UN, perhaps. The Commonwealth is sometimes seen as having developed in parallel with the UN, with which it is credited as having a stimulatory and cross-fertilizing role. Its members belong, of course, to the numerous UN committees, councils and commissions, as well as to the General Assembly and the two organizations co-operate in certain fields. But is the relationship a useful symbiotic one or merely an example of overlap? To raise such questions is not to devalue the usefulness and quality of some of the projects undertaken by the Secretariat. Its analysis and recommendations on the establishment of a new international economic order have been widely praised. Ramphal was a leading member of the Brandt Commission on North-South economic issues and has tried hard to place the Commonwealth in the forefront of the drive for a more equal distribution of wealth. Then there is the scheme for an open university, named by the historian Lord Briggs and his committee as the University of the Commonwealth for Co-operation in Distance Learning, with the aim of teaching students anywhere in the Commonwealth helped by existing colleges and universities. And, to take one more example, the study of the impact of climatic change and rising sea levels on a number of Commonwealth countries is particularly relevant to an organization which counts many island states and countries with low-lying coastal regions, such as Bangladesh, among its members.

The Secretariat's flagship agency is the Commonwealth Fund for Technical Co-operation, founded in 1971 and with a permanent staff at present of 124. It describes its job as 'providing technical assistance to all developing countries within the Commonwealth, not dispensing capital but injecting enterprise. It enables each country to draw upon the immense variety of the Commonwealth, and to offer its own skills to others.' Mostly it is technical co-operation between developing countries and in 1987 CFTC had more than 270 experts (70 per cent of them from developing countries) at work, while it supported nearly 2,800 trainees and students. There is an Industrial Development Unit doing what its title implies, and a Technical Assistance Group (TAG) which employs a small staff of specialists to provide consultancy services in such fields as law, economics, finance and computing. TAG's debt-management system, with its special software, has been taken up by 20 countries and is competing successfully with rival systems; the latest buyer is Thailand. Under CFTC's wing, too, come the Special Fund for Mozambique, the special fund to provide educational training for Namibians, and the Nassau Fellowship Fund for South Africans.

The CFTC, like so many Commonwealth institutions, is in trouble, however. Its funds, provided by Commonwealth countries on a voluntary basis, slumped in 1986–7, a year of financial crisis, according to its new Canadian managing director, Bill Montgomery. The staff have been cut and may have to be cut again. Administrative costs have risen to 18 per cent of expenditure, largely because of the sharp rent increases. Three factors have hit revenues: the general financial squeeze; the strong pound, which reduced the value of contributions paid in sterling; and the Australian decision to cut their contribution by one-third, in line with a general policy of shifting from multilateral to bilateral aid. Britain gets some of the blame. It was criticized by Ramphal in his report to the 1987 summit for insisting on limiting its contribution to 30 per cent of the total contribution from all Commonwealth countries. Insistence on this formula, designed to keep other countries up to scratch, had acted to CFTC's detriment; what was happening represented 'a weakening in Commonwealth multilateral efforts which must be of serious concern to all countries'.

During the 1970s the British were the biggest contributors to the CFTC. By the end of the 1980s that position was occupied by the Canadians, who give a fixed sum, and in 1988 were providing nearly 40 per cent of a planned expenditure of £23.2m. for 1988–9. Despite stepping down from first place among the donors, the British helped save the day during the 1986–7 crisis by raising their contribution to 34 per cent, although they gave notice that they would claw back the extra as soon as there was a chance. The Australians, too, eased their cut after listening to approaches from Ramphal and the Canadians, the champions of the Commonwealth spirit.

The story of the CFTC is a significant one. The Canadians use organizations like the CFTC not only because they are the Commonwealth's strongest supporters but also because they do not want to increase the size of their own aid bureaucracy in Ottawa. The British and the Australians, on the other hand, concentrate their aid in bilateral projects, which make it easier to control and sharpen the political focus. And British multilateral aid goes increasingly through the European Community's Development Fund. Arthur Kilgore and James Mayall have written[10] that CFTC's emphasis on technical co-operation among developing countries (TCDC in the acronymic jargon of the aid fraternity) is one reason for cooled British enthusiasm.

It tells us something about the character of the new Commonwealth that it has evolved a programme for the transfer of resources that is run on principles other than those on which British aid policy is currently based. The emphasis on TCDC can be interpreted as a conscious effort to loosen the transnational ties of dependency between the traditional metropole and the developing Commonwealth countries.

The next Secretary-General

Money, structural problems, establishing priorities, making decisions – such things matter only in relationship to whether there is a will to continue the Commonwealth, which means establishing a consensus on what it can do positively and uniquely. Uncertainty about its future has been endemic for at least three decades. Even Ramphal responds with a less than vibrantly optimistic 'Yes, I think so' when asked whether it will last into the next century. Whoever takes over from him in mid-1990 will find himself at the head of an organization which will need to have its functions redefined and its goals firmly established if it is to survive. Only one paladin has so far flung his hat into the ring and announced he is off and running: Malcolm Fraser, the Australian former Prime Minister and leader of the Eminent Persons Group whose mission to South Africa foundered in 1986.

Physically impressive, Fraser has the sort of patrician rancher's gloss which speaks of wealth, power and cloudless skies. In appearance and aura he is not, in fact, unlike the tobacco barons of Rhodesia whose negotiated downfall he helped engineer at the 1979 Lusaka summit. All came out of the same colonial settler mould. But Fraser has established his credentials as an enemy of apartheid and has also made it clear that Africa's one-party states are not beyond the democratic pale so far as he is concerned. He has no sympathy for Mrs Thatcher's view that time and demography will bring reform to South Africa and believes that she should have joined the rest of the Commonwealth in supporting comprehensive sanctions. South Africa will remain on the front burner at summits if he becomes Secretary-General and he would expect Britain to join the ranks of the sanctioneers in the interests of solidarity. 'Consultation should lead to commitment', he said at a 1988 Commonwealth seminar in Britain.

The determination with which he has lobbied for the job has surprised some people. 'He's always been a big fish and he can't bear being out of the swim', said an Australian politician who knows him well. 'He sees the Commonwealth as the best available way of getting back in.' 'If you're a rich farmer with nothing much to do, it doesn't look so bad as a job', said another Australian. Fraser has the backing of Bob Hawke, the Australian Prime Minister, but it is questionable whether he will get the crucial African vote despite intensive lobbying, including a trip to Dodoma, the rarely visited new capital of Tanzania, to meet Julius Nyerere, President Mwinyi and Salim Salim, the Zanzibari Deputy Prime Minister (a very competent diplomat with UN experience whom many would like to see stand for the Secretary-Generalship).

Fraser's chances were lessened towards the end of 1988 by the decision of the Nigerian leader, Major-General Ibrahim Babangida, to nominate his fellow countryman, Chief Emeka Anyaoku, the mild-mannered and cautious Deputy Secretary-General (Political) of the Secretariat. Anyaoku wants the job, but he is inhibited by his position in the Secretariat from campaigning publicly. Mrs Thatcher, who regards Fraser as a renegade Tory wet, rather like Brian Mulroney of Canada, and feels that Anyaoku has spent too long playing second fiddle to Ramphal, fancies neither candidate. The Secretariat staff, who have heard of Fraser's notoriously short-fused temper and impatient demands on his staff, would probably prefer almost anyone else. 'If Fraser has to get up at 3 a.m. to work, he expects the rest of his staff to get up with him', said an Australian diplomat, recalling just such an incident when Fraser was visiting Washington.

Whether or not he gets the secretary-generalship, Fraser is a significant Commonwealth figure, an Australian monarchist and the nearest thing there is today to a Commonwealth statesman in the tradition of Menzies (a hero of his). His efforts at reshaping and reinvigorating the Commonwealth have not always been successful. The idea which he promoted at the 1977 London summit of holding regional summits provoked spirited resistance from Ramphal,[11] whose opposition may have been partly inspired by fears that they would weaken the Secretariat's powers. The first regional summit was held in Sydney in the following year and Ramphal's fears were soon seen to have been exaggerated. Alan Renouf, former head of the Department of Foreign Affairs in Canberra, described the Sydney meeting as an 'international non-event' and a 'patent flop' whose main purpose had been to inflate Australian pretensions to greater importance on the world stage.[12] Renouf is clearly no friend of Fraser, but the regional summit idea did indeed soon fizzle out, despite the Prime Minister's claim that it was 'one of the most useful foreign policy initiatives ever taken by Australia'. No regional summit has been held since 1984 simply because there has been no demand for one.

Fraser represents the dilemma facing the Commonwealth as it gears up for the 1990s: does it need a high-profile activist who would carry weight internationally (considerably more weight than either of his predecessors), or should the next Secretary-General be a quiet, methodical administrator, more bureaucratic than political in his inclinations, like Anyaoku? And if there is a deadlock, who then? Not Ramphal, it seems. He has ruled that out and, anyway, he has a damaging lack of rapport with Thatcher, as Secretariat officials freely admit. It can at least be said with confidence that whoever gets the job is not going to have an easy time.

3

From Empire to Commonwealth

AT THIS point it is worth taking a step back from the Commonwealth's current situation to look at how a nineteenth-century Empire evolved into an association of independent states. That will be the subject of this and the following chapter.

The Commonwealth is often seen as a sort of rapidly concocted salve applied to the wound Britain suffered from the loss of empire after the Second World War. It staunched a haemorrhage of pride and confidence, cleansed a poisonous sense of failure and in a way vindicated the country's history. In the age of the superpowers Britain was still wanted, it could still lead and its beliefs and institutions remained of value to countries brought to independence in its traditions. The lessons learned from the defeat of the first Empire in the American Revolution had been engraved on the foundation stone of the second Empire, and now here was a third and last Empire, both curative and compensatory, and free. But the idea of the post-war Commonwealth as a hastily made contrivance is essentially unjust both to it and to the Empire's traditions. The stock from which it grew was remarkably strong and even venerable, the creation of a liberalizing, reformist trend. In spirit at least the Commonwealth has been with Britain since the early years of the nineteenth century, an alternative empire that developed around and within the soldiers' empire of colonial wars and military power, its roots planted firmly in the domestic soil of British politics, a survivor which outlived and to some extent destroyed its host.

'Kings and aristocracies can govern empire', said Lord Derby, the mid-nineteenth century Colonial Secretary and Prime Minister, 'but one people cannot govern another people.'

An empire which pledges itself to the rule of law and equal justice for all its subjects finds it increasingly hard to justify discrimination in the matter of rights. What it does abroad has to be consonant, more or less, with what it does at home. If the slaves abroad were emancipated in the Act of 1833, so, in the same year, was the lot of the industrial 'slaves' at home improved through the Factory Act. There was no conscious equation of the two reforms, of course, but in a wider sense their passage in the same year (or that they came a year after the 1832 Reform Act) was not coincidental. Nor were the remarks of Macaulay when defending the Government of India Act in the House of Commons in July, 1833, that it would be 'the proudest day in English history' if, at some future date, the Indians, having been educated into a capacity for better government under British tutelage, should demand European institutions.

The Empire may have been exploitative – a vast system of outdoor relief for the upper classes, as James Mill, the radical philosopher and father of John Stuart Mill, described it – but its masters only rarely regarded it as immutable. Progress was, after all, part of the imperial creed. It was, of course, an empire split down the middle between the settled colonies, such as Canada, and the colonies which had been conquered, handed over or whose people had sought British protection out of fear of worse masters. The first was 'family'. The other was an empire built on racialist lines in which Britons ruled Asians, Africans and other non-whites. India was the heart of this second empire, an empire in its own right, so exotic and culturally varied that it defied the prim, good-housekeeping brand of imperial accountancy. But there, as in other colonies in this class, the rulers stood apart and held on to their power and privileges. The ruled were ruled for their own good; and what that good was was decided by rulers absolutely confident in the moral and intellectual superiority of their own race and system. On that point there was not much difference between the Colonial Reformers (also known as Radical Imperialists) and the old-fashioned imperialists.

The word Commonwealth was not used to describe an evolving empire until late in the nineteenth century, coined by a Liberal Imperialist, Lord Rosebery, who was to support that very imperialist, and cathartic, struggle, the Boer War. The occasion was in Adelaide, South Australia, in January 1887: 'There is no need for any nation, however great, leaving the Empire, because the Empire is a commonwealth of nations', he told his audience in the context of considering the implications of nationhood.[1] As a vision it contrasted with Disraeli's Empire of the Queen, which focused on the Raj, but both had in common the weaving together of nationalism and the need for strategic defence in the face of increasing challenges from other imperial powers.

The commonwealth of which Rosebery spoke was, in reality, the white, settled dominions. Even in that penultimate decade of the nineteenth century it was not envisaged that India and a host of other colonial possessions, some treasured, some 'wretched burdens', would achieve statehood, with parliamentary institutions, in the foreseeable future. Despite the acceptance by Macaulay and others that Indians might one day be able to rule themselves through European institutions, it remained a fact that the Indian nationalists who in the latter part of the century clamoured for dominion status did not have much in the way of a receptive audience among the rulers. Rosebery's commonwealth was not entirely kith and kin, of course. There were French Canadians and Afrikaners, but they were white and, with the exercise of wise statecraft, just about assimilable. The distinction between the white dominions and the rest of the Empire remained even when the Commonwealth (with a capital C by now) was more closely and intellectually defined, and aligned with budding concepts of a League of Nations (there was often a fine line between the radical school of imperialism and internationalism) after the Boer War. The residual impression of a club membership composed of them and us remains in British minds today and has to be taken into account when considering the tensions and frustrations which have afflicted the present-day Commonwealth. The multi-racial ethic which is supposed to bind the two together may be noble but it is of only recent manufacture and none too effective.

The men who planted the Commonwealth idea in the 1830s were Colonial Reformers – Utilitarians, followers of Jeremy Bentham, radical in their willingness to think afresh and challenge the self-serving assumptions of the aristocracy and gentry, Tory or Whig. They were also Malthusians, deeply concerned with the demographic trends which produced overpopulation and unemployment in the towns as well as the countryside of early nineteenth-century Britain. In any case, the approaching end of the mercantilist, self-contained trading system, and the triumph of the new creed of Free Trade, meant (as a leading Colonial Reformer, Sir William Molesworth, pointed out) abandonment of the very reason why colonies were defended and cherished. If your assets cost more to maintain than they delivered in profit, why continue to waste the tax-payers' money on them? Such thinking made the Colonial Reformers open to ideas of self-governing colonies and the assisted emigration of free men (as opposed to the unfree ones who went in shackles to imprisonment and servitude in Australia). In that sense, they were more imperialistic than the majority of the English ruling class, among many of whom the alternative creed of Separatism was prevalent. They took the view that settler colonies were, one way or another, bound to become independent and would before long sunder themselves from the metropolitan power, as the 13 American colonies had done. More militant imperialists of the old school opposed any such devolution of authority. Responsible local government and the sovereignty of Great Britain were completely incompatible, the Duke of Wellington had declared thunderously.

A mood of imperial fatigue may have been around in the wake of the Napoleonic Wars, but the era was not, as some historians have claimed, anti-imperialistic. The soldiers' empire continued much as it had always done, as a look at the record between 1839, the year of the publication of the Durham Report recommending self-government for Canada, and 1850 demonstrates: 1839, Aden annexed, First Afghan War and First Opium War begins; 1842, Hong Kong ceded to Britain, conquest of Burma and Assam begins; 1843 Maori Wars begin, Sind conquered and Natal annexed; 1845, First

Sikh War; 1848, Orange Free State becomes a Crown Colony, Second Sikh War and annexation of the Punjab.

Durham and Canada

John Lambton, first Earl of Durham, was a Whig, not a Colonial Reformer or Radical Imperialist (he haughtily refused an offer to lead the group), but he was nevertheless their man as much as he was anyone's. The Commonwealth had its inception with his report, which is why it is worth taking a look at how it came about. It has characteristics of high-mindedness, racialism, benign intentions, confusion, bloody-mindedness and governmental indifference which are not unknown today in Commonwealth affairs. How far Durham was the true author has always been a matter of some conjecture. He was a very sick man, only a year away from death at the age of 48, when it was published. John Stuart Mill credited most of it to the two leading members of his team (Edward Gibbon Wakefield and Charles Buller, Durham's Chief Secretary), and the inspiration to John Arthur Roebuck, a Madras-born Member of Parliament of rather uncertain radicalism (he caused a stir in later years by championing the slave-owners of the Southern States during the American Civil War). Roebuck had flatly contradicted the Duke of Wellington, and those who thought like him, in a memorandum to Durham on the eve of his departure for Canada in 1838 in which he stated that 'the supremacy of England and the well-being of the colony are completely compatible'.[2] In his view, the separation of Canada from Britain would not be a calamity provided it occurred amicably and the colonies concerned formed an independent federation 'united in bonds of friendship with England' and were not added to the United States. He was anxious to stop the extension of the United States to the North Pole, a development which he considered would be 'fatal to the maritime superiority of England'. Quite why is not clear, but presumably he had in mind the control of the North-West Passage, an uncharted (and, as it turned out, impassable) sea-route with which the Admiralty was then preoccupied.

FROM EMPIRE TO COMMONWEALTH   39

In both Upper (Ontario) and Lower (Quebec) Canada there had been movements demanding reform which drew on the United States for inspiration. The uprisings they produced, led by Louis-Joseph Papineau in Quebec and William Lyon Mackenzie in Upper Canada, were put down in a couple of brisk skirmishes. The Whig Prime Minister of the time, Lord Melbourne, commissioned Lord Durham to investigate and make recommendations which would lead towards self-government not just for Upper and Lower Canada but for the Atlantic Maritime provinces as well. The main issue in Lower Canada, as Durham soon discovered, was the underlying conflict between English-speaking and French-speaking Canadians. As Durham reported in a famous passage: 'I expected to find a contest between a government and a people: I found two nations warring in the bosom of a single state; I found a struggle not of principles but of races.'

Durham was a millionaire of poor health and unstable temperament who was given to outbursts of incivility and even violence. In March, 1838, when he sailed for the St Lawrence aboard *HMS Hastings*, he had few friends and a considerable number of enemies. He had insulted his father-in-law Lord Grey, a previous Whig Prime Minister, at a cabinet dinner; Melbourne and Palmerston, the Foreign Secretary, disliked him; and he had a deadly enemy in his fellow Whig of a radical tendency, Lord Brougham, with whom he had quarrelled, basically over which of them was entitled to claim the greater glory for the passage of the 1832 Reform Bill. He was undoubtedly spoiled and too wealthy for his own good, as Brougham claimed. Nicknames abounded: 'Radical Jack' (for his part in the Reform Bill), 'The Angry Boy', 'Lord High Seditioner' (*The Times* at the time of his abrupt resignation in Canada) and 'The Dictator', the affectionate title given him by his hard-worked staff in Canada. His wife in her diary almost always gave pronouns referring to her husband a capital 'H'.

Above all, perhaps, he was ambitious and vain. 'Canada will one day do justice to my memory', are his dying words recorded on the fly-leaf of Stuart Reid's two-volume *Life and Letters*.[3] Canada, large as it already was, was not yet quite

sufficient as a monument, but he had hopes of it. As for the ambition, that had never been satisfied. He had held the office of Lord Privy Seal but had never presided over any great department of state. Canada was the summit and his report the exit line of his career.

Melbourne, as he ran into his first brush with Durham, might have appreciated the assessment by a later empire builder of a different sort of the unpredictability of vain men. Beware of them, Cecil Rhodes advised John Buchan, the author and also a governor-general of Canada. 'You can make your book with roguery, but vanity is incalculable – it will always let you down.'[4] It was the character of some of the people Durham took with him to Canada which dismayed Melbourne. Even the relaxed attitude adopted by today's prime ministers on matters of morals would have been strained by the choice of Edward Gibbon Wakefield, noted though he was for his brilliant ideas on planned settlement in South Australia and New Zealand. Most of these had come to him while he was serving three years in Newgate prison for the abduction of a 15-year-old heiress, his second such exploit. Fortunately for him, the marriage had not been consummated. Otherwise Wakefield might have missed Canada and found himself pioneering in the Antipodes rather earlier than actually occurred, with a sentence of 14 years transportation.

Melbourne's gloomy warning that 'if you touch G. W. (Gibbon Wakefield) with a tongs it is utter destruction, depend upon it', was disregarded by Durham, himself an eloper. He knew that what mattered most were the ideas and commitment Wakefield would bring to the venture. There were similar objections to Thomas Turton, on the grounds that he had been involved in an infamous divorce; Turton had been at Eton with Durham and had had a successful career at the Indian Bar. A third member of the team, Tommy Duncombe, a sporting friend of Durham, was, said Melbourne, 'not so bad, but he is of the same genus and can do nothing but harm'. Durham was urged to show 'respect and reverence' for the age and character of the young Queen who had approved his appointment, but he was unimpressed; in any case, regardless of the blemishes on some of his companions, his brief had already been agreed. As he told the House of Lords in a ringing farewell speech:

> I go to restore the supremacy of the law, to be the humble instrument of conferring upon the British North American Provinces such a free and liberal constitution as shall place them in the same scale of independence as the rest of the possessions of Great Britain, and as shall tend to their own immediate honour, welfare and prosperity.

The real question was how far his standing had been damaged and whether, by providing ammunition for his enemies, this would hamper him in attaining his goal.

Durham's downfall was brought about by too much magnanimity. On 28 June 1838, the anniversary of Queen Victoria's coronation, he granted an amnesty to almost all those who had taken part in the Papineau rebellion. Eight were exiled to Bermuda (without prior notification to the Governor of Bermuda or the British government). The amnesty was not extended to those, like Papineau, who had fled to the United States. The possibility of trials and sentences carrying the death penalty had been avoided. 'Not one drop of blood has been shed', he wrote to the Queen. 'The guilty have received justice, the misguided mercy.'

Durham was ill, depressed over the row about his subordinates, even before the news came, via the New York newspapers, that his ordinance had been disallowed in London. There had been a technical error: the men sent to Bermuda had not been tried, so how could they legally be exiled? argued Brougham, the lawyer, in Parliament. Ways of getting round that problem might have been found if there had been a will to protect Durham, but there was not. Melbourne, who had at first approved the amnesty, gave way. In those days of slow communication when officials were frequently obliged to act on their own judgment without consulting their governments, disallowance was not uncommon. Disavowal might have been a black mark on a career, but it was not necessarily a resigning matter. A man less vain, less ill and less rich than Durham might have sat out the storm. He found it humiliating and resigned.

On the day before he sailed for home Durham mounted the highest tower of Fort St Louis and brooded over the scene, a romantic figure wrapped in the heavy cloak which he habitually wore against the cold. He had spent only five months in Canada, most of the time in Quebec City. On one side was the great divide of the St Lawrence caused by the Ile d'Orléans, on the other the Plains of Abraham where Wolfe had won Canada for England. It would be easy to say that Durham had won a second victory, but it would not be quite true. What he did with his report was to begin a process which led to independence. One of the ironies of Durham's mission was the adoration he inspired in the French community during his stay in the colony (it was to vanish when his report was published). Buller, who had taken the French side against his chief in the early stages of the mission, wrote admiringly that Durham had from the first perceived their 'narrow and mischievous spirit' and made up his mind that no quarter should be shown to their 'absurd pretensions of race'. The report described them as 'an utterly uneducated and singularly inert' people without the ability to invigorate and elevate themselves. Canada was to be British, in Quebec as elsewhere.

I entertain no doubts as to the national character which must be given Lower Canada; it must be that of the British Empire; that of the majority of the population of British America; that of the great race which must, in the lapse of no long period of time, be predominant over the whole North American continent.

The attempt to preserve French Canadian nationality was a 'vain endeavour'. The report recommended the union of the two Canadas under a responsible cabinet government which would hold power only so long as it enjoyed the support of the majority within the legislative assembly. It was to be an 'Anglo-Saxon' government supported by a programme of emigration from Britain. In that stipulation lay the source of the racial friction that plagues Canada to this day. There was no talk of multi-racialism; several more stages had to be gone through during the next 120 years before that became the prevailing creed. Nevertheless, the liberalizing Commonwealth had been initiated and it was possible for the first time to envisage the progress of a colony from dependence to independence by peaceful constitutional means. No other empire had ever dared to think in such radical terms. Durham and his aides were reformers in the English tradition and they can justly be called the founders of the Commonwealth of independent nations which evolved throughout the nineteenth century and into the twentieth.

Canada was not to become the Empire's first dominion until 1867, nearly 30 years after the Durham Report, when all its colonies were drawn together into a confederation under the British North America Act. The threat from the United States had finally vanished with the Civil War. Only through union could the country develop on a continental scale, as the United States had done. But Canada's new status as a self-governing colony did not come about through enthusiasm on the part of the British Government for an empire evolving into liberty. On the contrary. 'They want to get rid of us', declared Sir Alexander Galt, the Canadian statesman, during a visit to London at the time.

Even Disraeli, the arch-imperialist of popular legend, wrote in 1866:[5] 'Power and influence we should exercise in Asia; consequently in Eastern Europe; consequently also in Western Europe; but what is the use of these colonial deadweights we do not govern?' The Canadians should be able to defend themselves, the African naval squadron withdrawn and the West African settlements given up to make savings with which to build ships and have a 'good budget'. Disraeli was to be concerned mainly with India. It was romantic, or 'oriental' as one critic described it. If a people could not rule India, a queen could; and he made Victoria Empress of India.

The new imperialism

Separatist views may have been latent among the Liberals and observable even in people like Disraeli, but they were not the views of the populace. More than 100,000 London working men signed a petition to the Queen in 1870 declaring that they had 'heard with alarm that Your Majesty has been advised to give up the colonies'. It would be better, they thought, if those who wanted to work in the Queen's dominions were helped to do so. The new imperialists were on the march. Professor C. A. Bodelsen, a twentieth-century historian of empire, has described as 'astounding' the change which took place at the end of the 1860s and in the 1870s:[6]

With a rapidity and completeness which seem almost incredible, the Separatist school practically vanished from the face of the earth and the Pessimists dwindled into an insignificant minority.

What one contemporary observer called the 'jingo hurricane' had still to break, but the winds were rising rapidly. Empire had become a popular and emotive issue, abroad as well at home. The colonies did not want to leave the fold even when they were given independence, it was discovered. They were attached to the idea of a Queen and a home country. In Britain, there was an angry reaction to the refusal of Mr Gladstone's government to finance the New Zealanders' suppression of the Maori uprising in the 1860s. There were German, French and Russian challengers to Britain's supremacy, all anxious to win slices of the colonial cake. Overpopulation in Britain was a stimulus to emigration to lands which had been brought a lot closer by the steamship and the telegraph. Disraeli rode the crest of a popular wave when he delivered his famous Crystal Palace speech at a Tory banquet in June 1872. It was the 'Empire of England' of which he spoke, it should be noted, not yet the British Empire. Scotsmen, Irishmen and Welshmen were not yet admitted to the ranks of empire builders, not even by Disraeli, a Jew by birth, possibly because they were classed as Celts. Writers on Empire such as Thomas Carlyle and Charles Dilke were candid in describing the imperial master races as, respectively, Teutons and Saxons.

If you look to the history of this country since the advent of Liberalism – 40 years ago – you will find that there has been no effort so continuous, so subtle, supported by so much energy, and carried on with so much ability and acumen, as the attempts of Liberalism to effect the disintegration of the Empire of England . . .

It has been shown with precise, with mathematical demonstration that there never was a jewel in the Crown of England that was so truly costly as the possession of India. How often has it been suggested that we should at once emancipate ourselves from this incubus! Well, that result was nearly accomplished. When those subtle views were adopted by the country under the plausible plea of granting self-government to the colonies, I confess that I myself thought that the tie was broken. Not that I for one object to self-government; I cannot conceive how our distant colonies can have their affairs administered except by self-government. But self-government in my opinion, when it was conceded, ought to have been conceded as part of a great policy of Imperial consolidation.

Consolidation meant imperial tariffs, the right of Britons (and not just those already resident in the dominions) to use the unappropriated lands which legally belonged to the Crown, reciprocal agreements with the colonies on mutual defence, and a representative council in London which would maintain 'constant and continuous' relations between the component parts of the Empire. For the next three decades it was to be the glamorised soldiers' empire which prevailed; the empire of chotapegs and the North-West Frontier, of Sanders of the River and Alan Quatermain, of the Fashoda Incident and the Jameson Raid. The 'Scramble for Africa' led to an unprecedented garnering of colonies in a continent which until the 1880s was regarded mainly as a place where, in order to protect the long sea route to India, it was necessary to keep a base at Simon's Bay in the Cape. 'Are we to attempt the creation of another India in Africa?' Sir William Harcourt, the chief Liberal critic of expansionism, asked the Foreign Secretary, Lord Rosebery. The answer in the end was to be 'no'. Canada was where the Empire's successor, the Commonwealth of Nations, was conceived but Africa, the stamping ground of the most strident form of nineteenth-century imperialism, was where it was destined to be born.

4
The South African Matrix: Ideals and Magnanimity

IN THE last decades of the nineteenth century the English (and, as already noted, they were 'English', not 'British', in their outlook) came to terms with the fact that they possessed an empire unsurpassed in its extent and variety. It signified wealth, opportunity, moral responsibility and evidence of the superiority of the English people, and it gripped the popular imagination in a totally unprecedented way. But ideas on how it should develop were as varied as English politics. There were several shades of federalists, radical imperialists, those who regarded federalism as idealistic nonsense, straightforward, old-fashioned imperialists and those who believed in something wider, an English-speaking union which embraced Britain, the white self-governing colonies and the United States. The last was eventually to overtake and overshadow the Commonwealth in the form of the transatlantic alliance, a development which ensured the survival of Britain – and the Empire – in two world wars. The radical Liberal Charles Dilke in his immensely successful *Greater Britain*, written in the second half of the 1860s, found that everywhere he travelled in English-speaking or English-governed lands 'the race was always one' in its essentials, even where 'other peoples had modified the blood'.[1]

The idea which in all the length of my travels has been at once my fellow and my guide ... is a conception, however imperfect, of the grandeur of our race, already girdling the earth, which it is destined, perhaps, eventually to overspread. In America, the peoples of the world are being fused together, but they are being run into an English mould; Alfred's laws and Chaucer's tongue are theirs whether they would or no ... Through America, England is speaking to the world.

Here was the making of a 'moral directorship' of the world. John Seeley, Professor of Latin at University College London, took up a similar theme, speaking of 'pan-Anglicanism' in a letter he sent to the founding conference of the Imperial Federation League in July 1884. He saw the movement for union as comparable to the struggles that had united Italy and Germany,[2] but he restricted it to the Empire, which he portrayed in his *The Expansion of England*, as being (with the exception of India) 'a vast English nation' now ripe for political union:[3]

When we have accustomed ourselves to contemplate the whole Empire together and call it all England, we shall see that here too is a United States. Here too is a great homogenous people, one in blood, language, religion, and laws, but dispersed over a boundless space.

The commonwealth envisaged by James Anthony Froude, biographer of Thomas Carlyle and editor of *Fraser's Magazine*, joined the Empire and the United States in a union. 'I hope and believe that a time will come when there will no longer be Englishmen and Americans, but we shall be of one heart and mind, and perhaps of one name.'[4] Lord Carnarvon, Colonial Secretary under Disraeli, sent Froude to South Africa in 1874 to explore the prospects for a rather less ambitious union, one between the two Boer republics and the English colonies in the Cape and Natal. Carnarvon had Canada in mind as a precedent, but it was a doomed undertaking. It required two Boer wars to bring about Union, and it is arguable that it might have been better for the black majority – certainly for those in the English-speaking colonies – if it had never happened.

Froude, for all his elegance of mind and writing, was a racist who found slavery 'innocent and even beneficent'. Perhaps that was one reason why he idealized the Boers, who had founded their republics in flight from the emancipation of their slaves. In his writings can be seen the beginnings of the romantic image of the Boers which coloured British attitudes towards them during and after the 1899–1902 war. They were the pastoral world which industrialism and avarice had destroyed in England, a people whose lives were governed by simple, religious values, who wished only to be left alone, free from the corrupting outside influences which entered the country when gold and diamonds were discovered. The English-speaking South Africans by contrast were 'pulpy endogens' (a type of plant which has no distinction between bark and pith). Of the Boer farmers with whom he stayed while journeying across the Cape, he wrote:[5]

They are precisely what their ancestors were two hundred years ago. The young ladies look as if they had stepped down out of van Eyck's pictures. The sons might have sat to Teniers. The big solemn old family bible lies on the hall table with the family register in it of half a dozen generations. Long graces precede and follow supper, said seriously, however, and listened to seriously, not yet by any means a humbug or a form. At dawn, you are roused by faint quavering notes of women's voices which settle into a morning psalm or hymn to begin the day with. The English rowdies hate, despise, and malign these poor people as behind the age. To me they appear by far the worthiest people in the colony.

The Milner legacy

It was not a view to which Sir Alfred Milner, British High Commissioner at the Cape, was to subscribe more than 25 years later. His preferred end to the Boer war would have been unconditional surrender, so that the country could be reconstructed from scratch. There was no room for compromise and the pro-Boer 'screamers' must not be listened to. His intention was 'to knock the bottom out of the "great Afrikander nation" for ever and ever Amen'.[6] But that was never achieved. Reconstruction was to be based on reconciliation, not demolition. 'We are good friends now', Lord Kitchener, Commander-in-Chief, had declared as the Boer leaders signed the peace treaty at Vereeniging.

The young men, Scots as well as English but all from Oxford, whom Milner, a Balliol man, gathered around him after the war to build the peace became known as the 'Kindergarten', a mocking reference to his German background. They took, on the whole, a broader and more generous view of the 'Afrikander nation' than their chief. One of them was John Buchan, who found that an evening in a Boer farm carried him back in memory to his native Lowlands in Scotland. Milner, he noted, had nothing of the countryman about him and was incapable of understanding the 'tortuosities' of the peasant mind, something that was essential in dealings with Paul Kruger, the Transvaal President.[7]

He was not very good at envisaging a world wholly different from his own, and his world and Kruger's at no point intersected. There was a gnarled magnificence in the old Transvaal President, but he saw only a snuffy, mendacious savage.

Milner's jaundiced view of the Boer character had nothing to do with solicitude for the black population. His main concern so far as ethnic groups were concerned was with the loyalty of the Uitlanders, the mainly British immigrants who had been drawn into the Transvaal by the gold rush and whose denial of political rights by the republic's government was to be the *casus belli*. They, like the Boers, depended on a cheap, subservient labour force. 'You have only to sacrifice "the nigger" absolutely and the game is easy', he had told his friend H. H. Asquith, the Liberal Home Secretary, with cynical relish in 1893.[8] It was only the government in London which quibbled about the clause in the Vereeniging treaty which left the question of votes for Africans until after representative government had been restored to the defeated republics. That, it was recognized, effectively meant 'never'. 'It would not be in accordance with the tradition of British policy in South Africa to use words implying a doubt whether any civilized native would ever receive the franchise', declared a senior Colonial Office official, H. W. Just. But that was as far as indignation went. Milner supported the wording of the clause and the Cabinet accepted it. There were more important matters than African rights to consider.

Milner was concerned, like Disraeli, with imperial consolidation, the bonding together of the Empire into a world force capable of dealing with the growing threat from its challengers, principally the empires of Germany and Russia. In the 1880s Britain had annexed Bechuanaland and an unclaimed part of the Indian Ocean coast between the Cape and Natal colonies to ensure that the Germans (who had already taken South-West Africa) did not achieve a common frontier with the Transvaal. By the early years of the twentieth century it was beginning to be recognized that a great test of strength with Germany lay ahead. In that context, black rights were a side issue which could not be allowed to threaten the prospect of achieving a united South Africa whose loyalty would guarantee the safety of the strategic Cape route to India. Milner's view of the 'ultimate end' in Southern Africa was of 'a self-governing white community, supported by well-treated and justly governed black labour from Cape Town to the Zambezi'. When the young men of the Kindergarten talked about racism they meant the distrust and prejudice between Boers and Britons. The union they helped to create kept a South Africa led by Afrikaners (the majority of the white population) in the Empire, and later the Commonwealth, through six decades and two wars, but ultimately it gave the whole country to an inward-looking Afrikanerdom which introduced apartheid.

Almost certainly, the Africans would have eventually lost whatever limited franchise they were given regardless of how the Vereeniging treaty was phrased. Nevertheless, the Africans were 'sacrificed' by Britain and a principle, or 'tradition', as Just called it, betrayed, and the spectre of that betrayal was to rise more than half a century later to haunt the deliberations of the new Commonwealth. The reconstruction that followed the Boer War produced a near-perfect irony, too, to accompany the spectre. It is in the smudged triumph of imperial statesmen over the embittered history of relations between Boers and Britons that the origins of a multiracial Commonwealth can be traced.

The Kindergarten had it in common with Durham more than 60 years earlier that they believed in self-government and union under parliamentary institutions, but they differed with him sharply on the question of accommodating a defeated race. There was no demand in their programme for the supremacy of the 'Anglo-Saxons' and no derision of the Afrikaners' 'absurd pretensions of race' or their 'narrow and mischievous spirit'. Instead, there was a supreme confidence that an imperial system which had bred democracy and parliamentary systems on the British model in first Canada and then Australia and New Zealand could wed Britain's South African colonies to the Boer states and contain their union within a liberal empire of free nations and free men. A cynic might note that while the Boers were not Anglo-Saxons they were at least 'Teutonic' and white and therefore, presumably, assimilable within the concept of a master-race, but the ideas shaping the twentieth-century empire were more generous and liberal than that.

Canada, Australia, New Zealand and Newfoundland (until 1931 a separate part of Canada) were formally entitled dominions at the 1907 Imperial Conference, and South Africa was to join them after union in 1910. In India the National Congress had been born in 1885, a British conception which sprang from the belief of a retired civil servant, A. O. Hume, and a viceroy, Lord Dufferin, that the country needed a political party through which the politicians could express themselves. One of its founders, Dadabhai Naoroji, felt able to say at its conference the following year:[9] 'It is our good fortune that we are under a rule which makes it possible for us to meet in this manner. We are freely allowed to speak our minds without the least hesitation; such a thing is possible under British rule and British rule only.' The Morley-Minto reforms of 1907-9 placed Indians in the supreme councils of the Indian Government and broadened the states' legislative councils, introducing communal representation among other things. The forward march of liberal ideas was not confined to 'Anglo-Saxons' and whites (except, of course, in South Africa).

Milner did not share the internationalism which some of his Kindergarten, notably Lionel Curtis, were to espouse in the League of Nations, the forerunner of the United Nations. He was an Empire Man, his political thoughts concentrated on the struggle to perfect what he saw (in 1908) as 'the greatest political entity in the world today'. But Curtis was the 'Prophet' of the Kindergarten, the nearest thing to a philosopher the Commonwealth has had. He was also the man who, in the words of L. S. Amery, another Empire Man, 'did more, by his indefatigable energy and persuasiveness, than any other one man to bring about South African union'.[10]

Curtis and his fellow member of the Kindergarten, Philip Kerr (Lord Lothian), founded *The Round Table* (still a respected journal of Commonwealth affairs) to promote Imperial federation. The method they had used in South Africa of establishing discussion groups to debate the country's future was adopted on a wider scale throughout the English-speaking Empire. Curtis went out to South Africa as a soldier, and like many others who fought in 'the last of the gentlemen's wars', he was impressed by the enemy's virtues in war and defeat. Louis Botha, one of the best of the Boer generals and the first Prime Minister of the Union of South Africa created in 1910, was, quite simply, 'the greatest man I have ever known'.

From union in South Africa grew ideas of greater and greater confederations, or commonwealths, of which the British Commonwealth was only one. Curtis's *The Problem of the Commonwealth*, published in 1916 during the First World War, urged the case for an imperial union with its own constitution, foreign policy and taxation for defence. Lord Elton, in *Imperial Commonwealth*, expressed his conviction that for two generations Curtis's 'philosophy of the Empire was the power behind the scenes'.[11] It certainly gave a stimulating jolt to ideas on the Commonwealth, but it was essentially unrealistic. The self-governing colonies had little interest in surrendering policy-making powers to an imperial super-government and there was no constituency of any importance in London for a commonwealth empowered to make decisions which Britain would be constitutionally obliged to accept. Curtis's ideas ballooned into *Civitas Dei*, published in 1934, an immensely long work based on deeply religious principles, which summarized all forms of government from the Stone Age to the mid-1930s. His ultimate earthly commonwealth was a world super-state modelled on the United

States with its own military forces and its capital in Quebec.

Beneath the rhetorical impasto of the ideas of Curtis and others lie the outlines of weaknesses which would in time break through and disrupt the master design of a federated Commonwealth. The first weakness was in defence, as Curtis himself recognized. One of his last (he died in 1955) recorded contributions was a comment on a Royal Empire Society report[12] in which he pleaded for a strengthening of Commonwealth sea and air communications, noting that the machinery of co-operation between 1919 and 1939 had not secured the common interests and purposes of the Commonwealth. The Second World War exposed the hollowness of imperial power. From then on the Commonwealth played a decreasingly audible second fiddle to the 'Anglo-Saxon' alliance between the United States and Britain. There could never be a fraternal relationship of that nature with the post-war Commonwealth's largest member, India. And that fact demonstrated something else about the Commonwealth: it was, and remains, essentially a two-tier organization divided on racial lines.

Imperial co-operation

The creation of the Union of South Africa may have laid a curse upon the future of the Commonwealth, but it gave it a remarkable imperial statesman in Jan Smuts, a Boer intellectual from the Cape. Kitchener had clinched the Treaty of Vereeniging by taking Smuts aside and telling him to accept the treaty as the Liberals would be in power in Britain in a few years and would restore representative government to the Boer states. Smuts knew enough about England to believe Kitchener's assurance. He had spent several years in England, studying law at Cambridge, and then at the Inns of Court, and in his youth, he had been an admirer of Rhodes. Smuts' part in crushing a pro-German rebellion in South Africa at the start of the First World War, his commitment to the British cause and his command of the imperial forces against the Germans in Tanganyika gave him a unique status in London. He arrived there in early 1917 to attend an imperial war conference which on the recommendation of L. S. Amery, with the backing of Milner, was to be translated into the imperial war cabinet.

With the holding of the first colonial conference in 1887, the year of Queen Victoria's Golden Jubilee, a step had been taken which was to lead, after a slow start, to frequent meetings between British ministers and colonial leaders. The self-governing colonies were advancing steadily under British institutions, if not always at the same pace. Canada had had a federal constitution since 1867 and New Zealand's six provinces had been combined in a self-governing unitary state since 1876. Progress towards federation was slow and uncertain in Australia, principally because of the huge distances and poor communications between its states, and it was not until 1901 that they were federated as the Commonwealth of Australia. By the eve of the First World War, the dominions were important enough to involve themselves actively in imperial defence.

A British public and leadership sickened by the stalemate in France found Smuts inspirational. He was feted and his views sought to an extent which surprised but brought out the best in him. Ideas flowed from him: on the conduct of the war in the Middle East and France, on the League of Nations – and on the Empire. He countered the federal ideas of Curtis and *The Round Table* with his belief that consultation among independent states would create a more durable and effective framework. This grouping of allies bound by common purposes would be called the British Commonwealth of Nations. 'We are not an empire', he told members of both Houses of Parliament at a banquet given in his honour on 15 May 1917. 'Germany is an empire. So was Rome, and so is India, but we are a system of nations, a community of states far greater than any empire which has ever existed.' This may have been a pragmatic approach, but within it lay the hint that there was within Afrikanderdom a hidden agenda for retreat from the wider, more liberal world which Smuts represented. 'Today South Africa belongs to us once more', D. F. Malan, the National Party leader, was to declare after his triumph over Smuts and the United Party in 1948. 'For the first time since union South Africa is our own and may

God grant that it always remain our own.'

However one views the history of the Commonwealth in the inter-war years it amounts to a dwindling of power as the authority once held by Britain was decentralized without any machinery being set up to replace it.[13] The patchy and generally unfavourable response of the dominions to Lloyd George's call for a show of military solidarity at Chanak, in the Straits of Gallipoli, where in 1922 a British force stood between Kemal Ataturk's victorious army and the Greeks of Constantinople, demonstrated that wartime solidarity could not be taken for granted in peacetime. The dominions had taken part in the peace negotiations and had become members of the League of Nations, but Britain had signed the 1919 Versailles peace treaty on behalf of the Empire, with the dominion signatures appended below. Only four years later Canada affirmed its independence in international affairs by making a bilateral agreement with the United States on fisheries. The imperial conferences of the 1920s prepared the ground for the 1931 Statute of Westminster, which formalized a situation which already existed *de facto*: the British Parliament would no longer legislate for a dominion except by consent and no law made by a dominion parliament would be invalidated on the grounds that it was repugnant to English law. Winston Churchill thought the Statute 'pedantic'. The Australians and New Zealanders did not adopt it until 1942 and 1947 respectively. As Menzies said, it was misguided to attempt to put in writing what was essentially a matter of the spirit.[14]

In trade, though, there was a formal strengthening of the bonds. In the protectionist atmosphere of the slump, the objections of British free traders were overcome and a series of bilateral agreements on tariff concessions were agreed at Ottawa in 1932. Coincidental or not, there was a marked improvement in trade during the period of imperial preferences, whose last trace today in British trade is the special concession made by the European Community on New Zealand butter exports to Britain.

The dominions encouraged Chamberlain's appeasement policy and anti-war feeling in Canada and South Africa (in the latter's case, pro-Nazi as much as anti-war) led to those two countries refusing to participate in the Imperial Defence Committee, a development which hampered discussion of joint defence policies at the last pre-war prime ministers' conference, in 1937. But when Britain declared war in September 1939 the dominions followed suit (with the exception of the Irish Free State, still a member of the Commonwealth at that time). Unlike August 1914, war was not declared on their behalf by the King. Parliamentary approval was not deemed a prior requisite in Australia or New Zealand; the Canadian Parliament approved a declaration of war without a division; in South Africa the Nationalist Prime Minister, General Hertzog, failed in a bid to keep the country neutral and was replaced by Smuts.

There was no imperial war cabinet this time and the prime ministers did not meet until May 1944, when in a communiqué whose declamatory tones indicated its drafting by Churchill, they rejoiced that they had done so in a spirit of unity which found its strength 'not in any formal bond but in the hidden springs from which human action flows'. The dominions sent more than 2 million men to the war, India and the colonies another 3 million, but the war marked the end of the Empire as a military entity of significance. Australia and New Zealand owed their survival to the United States, with which they concluded the ANZUS pact in 1951. Britain wished to be a party to it, but was excluded by the United States, which feared it might become entangled in the defence of British colonies. Britain and Canada joined the North Atlantic Treaty Organization.

The end of empire

Great empires die of indigestion, said Napoleon. Britain's died of anorexia: too little economic strength at the centre, too little authority, a lack of guns and ships, a lack of will. In April 1946 the prime ministers of Britain and the dominions met in London as the leaders of the British Commonwealth. When they next met, in October 1948, it was as the prime ministers of the Commonwealth, without the prefix. India had gained its independence; so had Ceylon and Pakistan. The

Dominions Office became the Commonwealth Relations Office, which absorbed the India Office. Turgot, the eighteenth-century French economist, and the nineteenth-century British Separatists had been proved right: colonies did drop off the tree like ripe fruits as they achieved self-government. Except that, in Britain's case, as colonies were hustled into independence whether they really wanted it or not during the post-war decades, it could be argued that here was a rare case of the tree abandoning the fruit.

But it is not British to write off anything in a hurry. Ruins are repaired and relics placed in museums. The monarchy, the most splendid relic of all, was established as Head of the Commonwealth. The idea planted by Lord Durham was still there and still growing. Much rapid change had occurred as a result of war, but in many parts of the Commonwealth the process of internal political development had been set in motion many years before. In India's case, the country's new ruler was that fundamentally British inspiration, the Indian National Congress.

If one looks for a symbol of change in Indian history one can find it in the six-year battle which rumbled on until 1923 between the co-architects of the new capital at Delhi, Edwin Lutyens and Herbert Baker, over the gradient of the road which runs between Baker's secretariat building, the head office of the Indian Civil Service, to Lutyens' Viceroy's House. The road climbs briefly but steeply up the low hill of Raisina, too steeply for Lutyens' liking, since it obscures the full magnificence of the Viceroy's House, the crown of the ensemble. Lutyens wanted the gradient eased so that his palace would dominate the view from the approach down the mall now known as the Rajpath; Baker opposed him, claiming that to change the gradient would wreck the unity of his Secretariat. Cost was the reason given for not accepting Lutyens' argument, but essentially the decision was political. The Secretariat's domination of the scene was proof, Lord Reading, the Viceroy, was told by a senior member of the Imperial Delhi Committee, that the babu or Indian clerk ruled India.[15] The importance of the Crown had receded; the bureaucrat now held the high ground. By 1931, when the Viceroy's House was at last ready for occupation, the power weighting had shifted again. The first visitor of significance entertained by the Viceroy, Lord Irwin (better known by his later inherited title as Lord Halifax) was Mahatma Gandhi in loin coth and ragged shawl, a person so improbable in such regal circumstances that the Viceroy's dogs sniffed around him in disbelief. A seditious Middle Temple lawyer posing as a half-naked fakir, fulminated Winston Churchill as the two saintly figures conducted a series of talks which culminated in the Delhi Pact and Gandhi's agreement to call off the civil disobedience campaign and attend the second Round Table Conference in London as the representative of Congress.

The movement to decolonize was to be surprisingly bipartisan in the post-war years, but Labour provided the approved ethical garb in which colonies were freed – or dumped. 'I want this British Commonwealth of Nations to divest themselves of every vestige of imperialism and domination, determined to show by their example how possible it is to organise a commonwealth on the basis of mutual aid and service' wrote George Lansbury in 1935 in the *Labour Shows the Way* series edited by Clement Attlee, who was to become prime minister with a landslide majority in 1945. 'Our ideal is self-government, democracy and socialism'.[16] It was Africa which was to provide a virgin proletariat for Labour theorists after the war. By 1963 when Fenner Brockway published *African Socialism*, a few doubts about the direction of the African experiment were surfacing. He admitted that in Africa the fact had to be faced that 'the democratic constitutions which accompany independence do not reflect the prevailing social development and require some authoritarian limitation if governments are to function'. Like Lionel Curtis, he was badly infected by federalitis, prophesying a United Socialist States of Africa by the end of the century. Africa, he concluded was 'now the most important, fascinating and significant scene of social – and socialist – transformation'.[17]

The wish-fulfilling delusions and apologetics of Fenner Brockway are such that one sneers merely by quoting him. Africa has not turned out like that. But it was not a delusion peculiar to Brockway and his fellows in that brand of socialism. It was gladly accepted at a great many political levels that a disinterested and generous act of statesmanship was taking place. It was part of the cherished belief that the new Commonwealth still enhanced British power and prestige because it had brought freedom to so many parts of the world, even if the reality in Africa was that it had brought one-party states of inadequate substance. Combined with the Special Relationship with the United States, it was what marked Britain out as not only different from but more important than the other European states. Britain's history was that of a great maritime and imperial nation and the British people still believed throughout the 1940s and 1950s that that was where their destiny continued to lie. Traces of that thinking can be found in Mrs Thatcher's contemptuous rejection of any suggestion from Brussels that as the Community waxes after 1992 the importance of national legislatures to the regulation of people's lives will wane. Europe is acceptable as a huge free market, but a federal Europe is not a British goal. The world is a wider place than that.

Political instinct and political thought shape one another, learning to co-exist despite contradictions, and that process can be seen in the changing attitudes towards Europe and the Commonwealth in the first post-war decades. A Foreign Office brief for the Anglo-American talks in London in 1950 concluded that there was little prospect of Britain being able to unite the Commonwealth as a single world power. The attraction of the pound sterling and the Royal Navy was now less than that of the dollar and the atom bomb. 'An attempt to turn the Commonwealth into a Third World Power would only confront its members with a direct choice between London and Washington, and though sentiment might point one way interest would certainly lead the other.'[18] The Commonwealth was being written off as an alternative, either on its own or in conjunction with Western Europe, to the Atlantic alliance. It nevertheless remained a potent force in the British subconsciousness. The rightness of instinct was invoked by Anthony Eden, then Foreign Secretary, in January 1952 when he explained to a New York audience why Britain would not respond to American pressure to play a leading part in the creation of the European Community.[19]

This is something which we know, in our bones, we cannot do. We know that if we were to attempt it, we should relax the springs of our action in the Western democratic cause and in the Atlantic association which is the expression of that cause. For Britain's story and her interests lie far beyond the Continent of Europe. Our thoughts move across the sea to the many communities in which our people play their part, in every corner of the world. That is our life: without it, we should be no more than some millions of people living on an island off the coast of Europe.

British history and Commonwealth obligations were again cited by Harold Macmillan in 1958 as the reasons why Britain could not join the European Community at its foundation the previous year. But the 1960s were to be the decade of negotiations on Britain's entry into the Community, finally achieved in 1972. They were also the decade of the 'Wind of Change' sweeping through Africa, a gale which blew a resistant South Africa out of the Commonwealth.

5

Nassau: The First of a Trilogy of Troubled Summits

MOST MODERN summits are over in a flash. A day for the run of bilateral meetings between heads of government, a day-and-a-half for bigger occasions, three days for a superpower meeting. Leaders like to see one another and, even more importantly in some cases, to be seen seeing one another. But it is a bad summit if the outcome has not been guaranteed successful, or at least uncontroversial, by hard work beforehand. There are occasions, of course, when momentous new developments suddenly and unexpectedly emerge, but even then no one hangs around. Among the exceptions to the rule of brevity are Commonwealth summits, which tend to be more in the nature of plateaux than pinnacles. It has to be a large stage to provide space for a turn-out of between 40 and 50 heads of government, all of whom will want to make speeches aimed at domestic audiences as much as at one another. Add to that the fact that there is still a touch of the jamboree about the big biennial summits. The tents are pitched, the flags raised; royalty will pass by in its open-topped Daimler.

It may be a sign of the times that the 1987 Vancouver summit was the shortest biennial ever held – a mere five days. In 1955 the leaders of the nine member nations (which then included the Federation of Rhodesia and Nyasaland as well as Pakistan and South Africa) were in session for 15 days. By 1965 they were down to nine days; in 1975 to eight; and in 1985 to seven. During the same period, the communiqués and declarations produced by the summiteers were undergoing a compensatory process: they were getting longer. The 1955 meeting's communiqué covers two pages in the Commonwealth Secretariat's compilation of summit statements;[1] 1965's extends to ten pages, 1975's is the same; but from then on the combined length of communiqués and accompanying declarations begins to take off. Nassau in 1985 produced 23 pages and Vancouver's output in 1987 was approximately the same. One reason for the increased wordiness is, of course, the expansion of membership, with each state wanting its favoured subject or subjects fitted in somewhere in the communiqué. Another is a desire to produce ringing declarations on the issues of the day. For example, 1981 produced the Melbourne Declaration on the need for dialogue (a favourite Commonwealth word) between North and South on a new international economic order, and 1983 gave birth to the Goa Declaration on International Security and the New Delhi Statement on Economic Action. Rajiv Gandhi was at work again in 1985 with the Nassau Declaration on World Order; and 1987 had the Vancouver Declaration on World Trade as well as the Okanagan Statement and Programme of Action on Southern Africa. Such declarations are highly perishable commodities even when they come from the most hard-nosed and relevant assemblies. It is difficult to think of many from the Commonwealth which have lodged in that small section of the public memory which caters for declarations.

Although the Queen has no official role at a summit, even as Head of the Commonwealth, she always undertakes a tour to coincide with the venue and during the course of the summit will meet all the leaders singly and collectively. The Secretary-General has his reception, too, to which he invites the media to meet the heads of government. Leaders rarely seen by the more metropolitan elements of the media flit across the scene, shyly evasive when captured, worried when no one takes notice of them. There are opportunities to sound out figures like Prime Minister Paias Wingti of Papua New Guinea on Melanesian solidarity in the South Pacific or President Albert René on the perennial question of whether the Seychelles really is going to become a marxist people's republic. These are the occasions, commendably frank and enjoyably convivial, when the Commonwealth is at its most endearing. The media, it should be said, usually enjoy CHOGMs (Commonwealth Heads of Government Meetings). The Empire bequeathed any number of beautiful or interesting spots in which to hold them: Melbourne, Delhi, Nassau and Vancouver, to take just the last four biennials. Most of the faces are familiar and, on the whole, friendly, the subject matter predictable and not too exacting, and there are usually one or two good stories (mainly of the 'Maggie at Bay' variety during recent years) to justify the cost of the trip.

Since little of real substance can emerge from a summit of around 45 States (not all members attend) where consensus is the rule, the Commonwealth conference tends to get a media coverage which relies heavily on atmospherics. 'Massive rows' brood on stormy horizons, tables are thumped by furious politicians, and peacemakers abound. Even the Queen occasionally gets dragged in inventively as a one-woman conciliation service. The proceedings of the conference are closed; speeches and exchanges are not broadcast, although speeches are usually distributed later. The media are contained in a communications centre nearby where they are fed twice a day with briefings by a Commonwealth spokesman or spokeswoman. Briefing on that basis is a delicate art, to say the least, and the summaries have to avoid partiality and too much candour. The red meat comes from the off-the-record briefings given by national delegations, which in practice means the Old Commonwealth countries and India. The rule is not invariable, but generally attendance at a national delegation briefing is restricted to reporters from the country concerned. Their spokesmen know when the newspaper and electronic media deadlines fall and they also know, if they are at all astute, what the home market is looking for. What is more, they can hand it out without fear of direct attribution. It is a situation made for news management, with the irresistible titbit thrown out right on deadline. A solution (or, at least, improvement) would be to open up the proceedings, with a closed circuit TV relay to the press centre. At one time it might have been valid to argue that such a move would lead to a loss of intimacy, but that hardly applies today.

In newspaper editorials about the Commonwealth an

apologetic little prefatory phrase often crops up to the effect that if it didn't exist, no one would need to invent it. That can, of course, be said about a great many international organizations. What exactly does the UN Conference on Trade and Development (UNCTAD) discuss at its summits (also of the bumper variety) that is not better and more effectively discussed in more specialized meetings? Or the Non-Aligned Movement, for that matter? Need has never been an essential requirement for institutional existence, but if it is not there some issue will lodge and grow amid the empty spaces. Racism in South Africa is the issue which has taken over the Commonwealth. Just how damaging an important issue can be to an organization which has neither the capacity nor the mandate to handle it could be seen at the three summits held in the two years between October 1985 and October 1987. The first was the biennial in Nassau, the second the 'mini-summit' on South Africa which brought the leaders of seven countries together in London, and the third the Vancouver biennial. The cast was large but most of it acted as chorus to the main players: Margaret Thatcher of Britain, Bob Hawke of Australia, Brian Mulroney of Canada, Rajiv Gandhi of India, Kenneth Kaunda of Zambia and Robert Mugabe of Zimbabwe. During this period Gandhi and Mugabe were, in succession, chairmen of the Non-Aligned Movement (which, like the Commonwealth, has gnashed ineffectively at apartheid, not least at the movement's 1986 summit in Mugabe's capital, Harare), so both had an almost statutory obligation to be at the sharp end in the sanctions battle. Kaunda was the veteran of the group, the longest serving leader (since 1964, the year of Zambia's independence), a chairman of the Organization of African Unity and a pivotal figure among the Front Line States.

A graduate of the old school of colonial negotiation, he believes in an emotional, no-holds-barred approach when dealing with British politicians and diplomats. In his political prime, when Rhodesia was the all-absorbing issue, they had been sensitive to accusations of racism, selling out to mammon and threats to leave the Commonwealth. Ghana and Tanzania had actually left for a while after UDI in 1965. Kaunda was to learn only slowly that Mrs Thatcher feels no guilt about colonialism; if the truth were known, she probably thinks it was rather a good thing. But perhaps the cross-over point in British attitudes towards the African Commonwealth came in 1976 when a Labour government broke off relations with Amin's Uganda over the murder of Dora Bloch following the Israeli raid on Entebbe to free the hijack hostages. This was the first and so far the only time a British government has broken diplomatic relations with a Commonwealth country and, suitably enough, the decision was made in a unique manner. Anthony Crosland, the Foreign Secretary of the time, scandalized his senior officials by putting the matter to the vote at a Foreign Office meeting of officials (some quite junior) and ministers. Sir Michael Palliser, the Permanent Under-Secretary, was strongly opposed to the breach on the grounds that Uganda was a Commonwealth country and breaking off relations was rarely a good idea, anyway. The meeting split evenly when Crosland took the vote and he was obliged to cast his deciding vote in favour of the breach.[2]

Mulroney was the only one who really needed to run up the flag at the Nassau summit; the Commonwealth matters politically in Canada, or, at least, it matters to its foreign policy (see Chapter 7). But he and Hawke had in common the political reality that, whatever the strength of their personal feelings on the subject, the widespread aversion to apartheid in their countries meant that there was considerable mileage to be gained from a vigorous promotion of sanctions delivered from the Commonwealth stage. For Thatcher on the other hand, with her instinctive understanding of the nationalist underpinnings of populism, standing alone against a group whose subliminal image among the domestic constituency was one of a coarse mix of black despots, hypocritical Indians and assorted leftists was likely to do her more good than harm, provided the situation did not slide over the edge into a disaster in which there were mass resignations.

South Africa had not loomed large at the Delhi summit in 1983. It was the American intervention in Grenada which caught the attention there, producing a notable split between the African and Afro-Caribbean states. The Africans, led by Mugabe, opposed the intervention on quasi-ideological grounds (US capitalism versus opponents of US capitalism).

The Afro-Caribbeans, who were considerably nearer the scene, supported it for sound pragmatic reasons, among them a desire not to tread the Maurice Bishop road to martyrdom (or even to find themselves in a position where a Maurice Bishop could oust them from power, for that matter).

The great South African debate

At Nassau, however, the scene was set for a debate on South Africa which would unite all behind sanctions. The breeze rustling the palm fronds, the gentle surf hissing on the sands below the Cable Beach and Royal Bahamian hotels would soothe away differences. Hawke, still in Canberra, was reported as being in a state of mind 'where he can't wait to get his bum on the seat of the RAAF VIP jet taking him to the Bahamas'. The Commonwealth 'magic' would work, even on the obdurate Thatcher. As a conciliatory gesture, some of the sanctioneers, notably Hawke, hinted that they would not demand comprehensive sanctions and were prepared to settle for selective ones.

The only immediately visible unpleasantness from which most of the arriving leaders averted their eyes was the scandal surrounding their host, the urbane and mellifluous Sir Lynden Pindling, Prime Minister of the Bahamas since 1967, Privy Councillor, lawyer and twice chairman of the Commonwealth Parliamentary Association. The Bahamas, only a few minutes flight from Florida, have been synonomous with drugs and fugitive financiers throughout most of his time in office. A Royal Commission set up to investigate drug trafficking and corruption had raised questions about a large unrepaid bank loan to Pindling as well as about the huge sums of money which drifted through bank accounts in islands where the main visible forms of employment were tourism and the manufacture of straw hats. The opposition was out in force, harrying the Prime Minister with 'The Chief is a Thief' banners. Since then other allegations involving Sir Lynden and events in the early 80s have surfaced; in Jacksonville, Florida, 'Mad Dog Merkle', the noted prosecuting attorney, has been reported to have 'set his sights' on him following evidence given in the successful trial of a Colombian cocaine smuggler described as 'the Henry Ford of drug trafficking'.[3] Why Sir Lynden had been chosen as the host, and therefore chairman, of a conference where drugs would be among the significant items on the agenda was to remain a mystery. Ramphal came to his rescue at a meeting of the Commonwealth Press Union with a warning that Pretoria's disinformation department was at work, seeking through a host of 'paid and unpaid' agents in the media to denigrate one whose active opposition to apartheid had discomforted the regime. It was an attempt to strike at 'the core system of human values'.

The prologue to a summit is the Secretary-General's report for the intervening two years since the previous meeting. These reports are quite substantial documents, usually of more than 100 pages, covering a wide range of issues. South Africa had pride of place, right after international affairs, in the pre-Nassau report. At that stage the emphasis was certainly not on Commonwealth mediation, however. The summary of contents under the section heading read: *South Africa still blocking Namibian independence – Apartheid facelift masks new repression – Moves to beat South African propaganda – Gleneagles bites deep into apartheid sport – Training for Namibian and South African refugees*. Ramphal put matters more succinctly in his introduction to the report, *A Testing Time*: The Western Contact Group on Namibia had virtually faded away and the American policy of constructive engagement was in disarray; acceptance of South African good faith over Namibia was misguided; sanctions had to be contemplated to force South Africa to 'recant'. With Britain in mind, he repeated more or less what he had said in May at the annual conference of the International Defence and Aid Fund for Southern Africa (see p. 23); it was 'unthinkable' for any Commonwealth country to offer comfort to South Africa at this time; if the Commonwealth was to be true to itself, it had no option but to be in the vanguard of the final push against apartheid. 'Neither kinship nor vested interest nor an unspoken ambivalence to change in South Africa nor unwarranted acceptance of Pretoria's good faith nor mistaken perceptions of South Africa as an ally must obstruct a worthy

Commonwealth response.'

The serious weakness in this approach was that the imposition of sanctions was not to be carried out on a basis of shared sacrifice. There were only two Commonwealth economies which would be affected by a commitment to sanctions which would really hurt South Africa, the British harmfully and the Australian beneficially, since a rival exporter of minerals would have been pushed off the trading map. None of South Africa's neighbours was in a position to apply sanctions, regardless of what their leaders might say or what they were prepared to append their names to. The British had always questioned the benefits of political change brought about by breaking the back of the South African economy. In their view, chaos might well succeed racial tyranny with something even worse than the Group Areas Act and the violent repression of any threat to the status quo. After all, the types of government that had emerged elsewhere in Africa, including Kaunda's Zambia, did not provide grounds for believing that change would necessarily be the same thing as progress. In that case, why risk creating a situation which could well see the loss of nearly £3 billion in investments (the 1984 book value, and considerably reduced in succeeding years by disinvestment), 250,000 jobs (a somewhat suspect government assessment of how many British jobs depended on the South African connection), and the flight to an already overcrowded United Kingdom of up to one million refugees entitled to British passports?[4] Better to let the South Africans try to find their own way to salvation, prodded along by a mixture of internal and external pressures that would hurt but not destroy.

The British stake in South Africa is important to the British economy, but it is declining, as a look at the trade figures shows. In 1980 British exports were worth £998m. and imports £752m. The 1986 figures (which do not take account of inflation) were, respectively, £850m. and £829m. The South African trading relationship is nevertheless considerably more important to Britain than that with Nigeria, the biggest economy in black Africa. Exports to Nigeria in the 1980–86 period dropped from £1,192m. to £566m. while imports rose from £144m. (an exceptionally low figure) to £329m.[5]

Throughout the 1970s, while the oil price boomed, Nigeria had been in a position to threaten and punish Britain; by the time of the Nassau summit, in 1985, its economy was on the rocks. None of the other African sanctioneers mattered more than a small bag of beans so far as the British economy was concerned; and all were heavily dependent on aid. British investment in South Africa, despite its decline, was greater than in the whole of the rest of Africa, non-Commonwealth as well as Commonwealth. If one looks at another measure, the percentage of Britain's overseas investment in Commonwealth countries, that, too, showed a sharp drop, from 45 per cent in 1974 to 31 per cent in 1984.[6] Mrs Thatcher was not required to play her cards at Nassau in response to economic threats, but if she had been, she held a strong hand.

Ramphal's plan, supported by other sanctioneers, may have been merely to start a slow but irresistible movement towards comprehensive sanctions by Britain, augmenting those which already existed on arms, oil, computers, police security equipment and so on. But, by what can only be seen as miscalculation, he had set the Commonwealth on course for a failure the extent of which would become more apparent later on. Lord Home, a former Conservative Prime Minister and Commonwealth Relations Secretary, was to take him to task the following year over the meaning of the Agreed Memorandum which established the Secretariat. 'The Government should resist any attempt to turn the Commonwealth into an executive instrument of policy', he wrote in a letter to *The Times* published on 8 July 1986, echoing a clause in the Memorandum declaring that the Secretariat should not arrogate to itself executive functions. More importantly, perhaps, Ramphal had revealed what everyone knew but which it might have been better not to parade in public: that the Commonwealth has no real political centre and is not a relationship which matters more to any member than other relationships or interests. Thatcher was to demonstrate that the European Community was the workshop in which she forged policy on an issue like South Africa and apartheid, and that the opinions of Commonwealth countries, either singly or collectively, were of secondary importance.

By revealing that the emperor had no clothes, Thatcher also, of course, revealed that neither had anyone else in the Commonwealth, apart from herself. The place was a veritable nudist colony. To be unwilling to strip in such a situation does not make for popularity, as she was to discover at Nassau and subsequent summits.

Pleas, cajolings and threats of catastrophe failed to move her as the summit plunged into the South African quagmire. Gandhi urged that the Commonwealth should not be seen as brave in words and cowardly in action; it had to demand mandatory comprehensive sanctions. Kaunda, the Cassandra of the summits, warned that the end was nigh: 'An explosion is imminent which will blow up everything – hundreds of thousands of people will go with it.' Thatcher responded by asking if any of them would negotiate with a gun at his head. The leader of the Nigerian delegation delivered the traditional threat of economic reprisals if Thatcher did not agree to sanctions, but it was brushed aside and ignored; the Nigerians no longer possessed muscle of that sort.

Meanwhile Hawke, in alliance with Mulroney, was well advanced with a proposal for mediation which would temporarily take the heat out of the sanctions battle. The Commonwealth would send a team of Eminent Persons to Southern Africa to encourage a political dialogue between the opposing parties. A muddled British briefing, based on faulty information from Sir Robert Armstrong, the Cabinet Secretary, inadvertently disclosed that the British saw themselves as the most effective mediators. History had given them that role and, as with the Rhodesian settlement, there was resistance to the idea of the Commonwealth becoming deeply involved. It was, after all, the Commonwealth which had expelled South Africa from its ranks against Macmillan's objections; offers of mediation from that direction were unlikely to be received with humble gratitude in Pretoria, particularly when they were accompanied by threats to squeeze the life out of the economy if power was not passed to the majority. The idea was not welcomed by the African National Congress, either. Its representative in Nassau, Mr Johnstone Makatini, Head of the ANC's International Department, described it as 'like trying to arrange a duel between a whale and an elephant – there is no meeting place'.

The leaders retired to Lyford Cay, a millionaires' haven a few miles from their hotels, for the weekend. Thatcher's spokesman, the choleric and usually extremely astute Bernard Ingham, returned from this luxury battlefield to report 'It's hard pounding down there, but she's not giving an inch'. And, indeed, by her own estimation, Thatcher did not give an inch. The concessions she made for the eventual agreement that at least put off the day of universal reckoning were minimal, peanuts by comparison with the golden nuggets of South African trade. Holding thumb and forefinger of her right hand fractionally apart for the benefit of press and television, she managed to be both winsome and gloating as she emphasized that she had given away only a 'tiny little bit'. The list of agreed sanctions included only three that Britain had not already imposed on its own or under the aegis of the European Community: a ban on the import of krugerrands (a small item in British trade), a ban on government-to-government loans and a stop to government funding of trade missions and participation in South African trade fairs and exhibitions. There was no record of British government-to-government loans ever having been made in the past and the amount spent on South African trade fairs and missions in 1984–85 came to £186,000.

The most important part of the accord was the decision to set up an Eminent Persons Group whose members would be selected by seven countries. Its main purpose was to initiate, in the context of a suspension of violence, a dialogue with the goal of creating a non-racial and representative government. This would involve the dismantling of apartheid, the unconditional release of the imprisoned black leader Nelson Mandela, and the lifting of the ban on the African National Congress and other opposition political parties. If, at the end of six months, progress was deemed inadequate, the heads of government of the seven countries – Australia, the Bahamas, Britain, Canada, India, Zambia and Zimbabwe – would consider a further list of 'measures' (Thatcher had taken exception to the use of the word sanctions). These included inter alia bans on air links with South Africa, on its agricultural exports, on new investments and reinvestment of profits, and on the promotion of tourism. There was no binding commitment to implementation; 'some of us would . . . consider' imposing the measures, said the accord.

Ramphal proclaimed the accord a 'Commonwealth victory', and Hawke declared that 'disaster' had been averted by Mrs Thatcher backing down. Otherwise, there would have been the 'very distinct possibility' that the summit would have gone ahead with the accord without British participation.

'A classical international negotiation', said Ingham in summation; he spoke in a tone of profound satisfaction. It was a revealing phrase. Does one, for a start, hold a 'classical international negotiation' in a club? That is how the Commonwealth has always seen itself, a sentimental view, perhaps, given the stridency of some meetings, but nevertheless one which had value in that, like a club, the bonds were flexible, the mood tolerant. Yet here was the British Prime Minister's spokesman putting the Commonwealth on the same level as, say, the European Council in stormy session over the agricultural budget. The implication was that the Thatcher administration no longer regarded the Commonwealth as a club, much less a family, which some kindly souls insist is the better description. The distance between London and the rest had grown a little wider. Thatcher had treated the Commonwealth as if were the European Community, where skins are thick and muscles hard, the issues relevant and not the flimsy scenery of dreamland. She had allowed it to be saved by the bell and was now prepared to forearm and necklock the stuffing out of it in the second round before allowing matters to proceed to a foregone conclusion in the third.

6

Through Pretoria to Vancouver

AFRICA SOUTH of the Zambezi is littered with the tombstones of missions that have set out in the belief that the wilderness trails will lead them to a High Priest aware that the old gods have failed and secretly yearning to hear the message of mercy and peace that they bring. Two such missions were mounted in 1986 and both perished miserably. The maps were wrong and the High Priest cruelly dismissive.

The first was the Commonwealth Eminent Persons Group, agreed in principle at Nassau. Bob Hawke, the originator of the idea, gave the co-chairmanship (and, effectively, the leadership) to Malcolm Fraser. The other co-chairman was Gen. Olusegun Obasanjo, an ex-military ruler of Nigeria who had redeemed himself by leading the country back to civilian rule, though only for a brief interregnum. The other members of the group were Lord Barber of Wentbridge, chairman of the Standard Chartered Bank (which at that time held 38 per cent of the equity of the Standard Bank of South Africa), and a former Chancellor of the Exchequer in the Heath government; Dame Nita Barrow from Barbados, a President of the World Council of Churches; John Malecela, former Foreign Minister of Tanzania; Sardar Swaran Singh, former Indian Foreign Minister; and Archbishop Edward Scott, Primate of the Anglican Church of Canada. The group was complete by the end of November 1985 and, following a reconnaissance in February by Fraser, Obasanjo and Dame Nita, made two trips to South Africa as a full group in March and May 1986.

The group was more successful in terms of atmospherics

and access to the South African leadership than most people had expected. They had 21 meetings with ministers, including President Botha, saw Nelson Mandela twice in Pollsmoor prison, Cape Town (in addition, Obasanjo saw him in February on his own), and, in the course of their travels outside South Africa, were able to talk at length with the African National Congress leadership and most of the leaders of the Front Line States. 'Pik' Botha, the South African Foreign Minister, was politely encouraging, listening to their proposals for the release of Mandela and legalization of the ANC in return for the latter ending its sporadic guerrilla war and using its influence to halt the township violence. He declared he was much impressed by Obasanjo. Here was a man whom experience of Nigeria's turbulent racial and religious mix had made sympathetic to Pretoria's theology of the multi-ethnic state. He understood the 'realities of Africa' unlike the 'do-gooders' of Europe and America.[1] It was a familiar South African tactic in dealings with black Africa: tell 'em we're all Africans and understand one another. Keep the rest out of it, eh?

Obasanjo described his special meeting with Mandela in a talk he gave to the Royal Commonwealth Society in London in September 1988.

I was accompanied by a prison officer of the rank of major-general and on the way he made some remarks for which I was totally unprepared. In a very earnest tone, he appealed to me not to misunderstand him. He had nothing against Nelson Mandela; he was merely carrying out his duties and if by some quirk of fate, Nelson Mandela were to become the President of South Africa the next day, he would willingly and loyally serve under him. It was only after I had met Mandela that the full significance of the major-general's remarks dawned on me. If the long period of incarceration was meant to break his spirit, it had patently failed to achieve its objective. There he was, tall, dignified and exuding grace and confidence. He was wearing a broad belt boldly painted in the colours of the ANC. Watching the deference of his gaolers towards him, it would have been difficult to know who was whose prisoner if one did not know that beforehand. It is in this light that what appears to be his creeping release by the regime should be seen.

A gentle mist of euphoria began to envelop the EPG as it shuttled hither and thither, avoiding the press as much as it could. But on 15 May President Botha scorched the mist away like a fierce sun rising over the Platteland when, in a speech televised nationally, he condemned the 'unsolicited interference' of 'meddling groups visiting the country'. Afrikaners who had begun to worry whether the government was going soft on the ANC were further consoled four days later when raids were launched against ANC targets in Harare, Gaborone and Lusaka (which the EPG had just left, after talks with the ANC, en route for South Africa). The Commonwealth mission was dead if not yet buried. An irony of the situation was that the ANC would have had to quiet the fears of its supporters by itself writing off the mission if Botha had not moved first. Reports of Pretoria's supposedly conciliatory mood had bred fears that the ANC was being led into a trap. Ramphal worsened his relations with the British Government by taking a strongly-worded slam at Thatcher in a statement which received little publicity amid the general furore: 'Those who are supine now must never speak again in righteous terms in the name of justice, morality and freedom; especially those whose policies help apartheid.'

The EPG's obituary, *Mission to South Africa: The Commonwealth Report*, was ready by mid-June. It called for comprehensive sanctions as 'the last opportunity to avert what could be the worst bloodbath since the Second World War'. The first printing ran to 55,000 copies and two others followed. The mission was at least a publishing success.

The Howe mission

The failure of the EPG gave the British a chance to do what they had wanted all the time, which was to mount their own expedition to Pretoria with the backing of the European Community. Britain was due to assume the Presidency of the Community in July for six months and Sir Geoffrey Howe would travel in the name of the 12 member states. No more woolly Commonwealth nonsense; this was the real thing and

Pretoria would have to sit up and listen. Thatcher, in alliance with Chancellor Kohl of West Germany, was able to persuade the Hague European summit in June to give Sir Geoffrey a short-duration licence of three months in which to talk to the South Africans; if nothing was achieved, then a package of sanctions involving minerals and gold coins could be introduced. The reaction by the Commonwealth sanctioneers to the Howe mission was hostile; it was seen as a futile attempt to persuade Botha to provide Thatcher with a few tokens of reasonableness which she could present as proof of progress when the Commonwealth mini-summit met to review the EPG mission. Pretoria had demonstrated that it would not listen to words or reason, said Fraser, and it was now 'impossible' for Thatcher to reject sanctions. 'Nobody can guarantee that sanctions will work, but words won't. Short of war, sanctions are the only weapons left, and without them Britain and America will have no weapons left in Africa.'

As soon became apparent, several of those who mattered in South Africa were not particularly anxious to see Sir Geoffrey. President Botha found the first date offered 'inopportune', and the ANC, Nelson Mandela, his wife Winnie, and Bishop Desmond Tutu all refused to talk to him. It was uncertain whether Mugabe would be on hand when he dropped in on Harare (in the end he was). The only people who really wanted to meet him were Kaunda and President Machel of Mozambique, and, as it turned out, their reasons were rather different. There were to be two trips within the space of one month, July, the first to Zambia, Zimbabwe and Mozambique, the second to Pretoria, with excursions to Swaziland, Lesotho, Botswana and, once again, Zambia.

It is curious how easily British politicians lose touch with the realities of white politics in Southern Africa; wishful thinking settles like a grey fluff over policies. It is hard to imagine a turn-of-the-century proconsul like Milner travelling from the Cape Town High Commission to Pretoria in an attempt to reason with someone like Botha; his on-the-spot appraisal of the Afrikaner character did not encourage a belief that Afrikaners were reasonable people. The whites of South Africa may live in one of the world's most beguiling climates, but they rule in no one's interest but their own and their political environment is accordingly hostile and dangerous. A politician like Botha wins power because he is not going to hand over the keys to the citadel of white interests; his supporters depend overwhelmingly on the state for employment, therefore the state must remain in their hands. They are, in fact, the state – the ticket collectors, the policemen, the civil servants, the soldiers. Sixty per cent of Afrikaners of working age are employed in the public sector. If there is a change in the system and blacks rule the country, their jobs will go to blacks.

Radical changes do not come about in such a system because of a conversion to liberalism. It was eight years of war and the slow erosion of sanctions and falling commodity prices which brought white Rhodesians to the negotiating table, not a sudden acknowledgement that only their injustice stood in the way of multi-racial harmony and prosperity for all. Negotiation is defeat, and the whites of South Africa know that as surely as Ian Smith knew it at Lancaster House in 1979 when Rhodesia signed the terms of surrender to Zimbabwe. The pace of change is that of a laboured forced march, at best an escape from sudden catastrophe. There are no quick breakthroughs for the mediators.

Thatcher and the good-natured Howe were persuaded to believe that an understanding approach to Botha from a British government that had buffered South Africa against comprehensive sanctions could break through the shell of Afrikanerdom's inward-looking rectitude and quickly produce results – such as the release of Nelson Mandela – which could be presented to the Commonwealth as evidence of progress. They were not calling for one-man-one-vote as the goal of reform; they were looking towards an eventual system in which power would be shared between the communities, so their ideas were at least broadly in tune with Pretoria's multi-ethnic philosophy. However, in Pretoria's book multi-ethnicity did not mean handing over power to the majority; it meant segmenting the majority on tribal lines and leaving central control of the country in the hands of whites. And just as importantly, it was an arrangement to be arrived at internally, not through outside pressure and advice. Any signs that the government was buckling at the knees would merely be weapons in the hands of the already resurgent extreme right-wing parties.

Thatcher was to maintain the belief that London had a special understanding with Pretoria for some time after a disillusioned Howe had abandoned it. Botha had come to Chequers for talks in 1984 and she entertained the idea of a brilliant gamble, a long flight south under the great mindless bubble of the African sky to see him again and tell him that coming to terms with the inevitable was not the same thing as appeasing his enemies. She considered it as a possible diversion from her itinerary when she visited Kenya and Nigeria at the beginning of 1988, and then, wisely, decided it would achieve nothing. The time was still not ripe when she visited Zimbabwe in April 1989, although she did pay a brief visit to Windhoek, the Namibian capital.

The traditions of diplomacy, though, are those of men inclined to see history as a seamless negotiating process. The failure of missions, the breakdown of negotiations, even wars are mere garbles in the fabric. At some point everyone comes back to the table. That's what the world is, one big negotiating table. So in a philosophical sense there was comfort for Sir Geoffrey as he boarded his RAF VC10 with his team of Foreign Office officials. Within the expanses of a historical process getting the bum's rush out of Lusaka and Pretoria was not going to seem all that important. Merely embarrassing, and what politician can't live with embarrassment, so long, of course, as it doesn't turn into downright humiliation? Sir Geoffrey is not a man who is easily humiliated. He enters into diplomatic ventures in a mood of temperate optimism, and on the VC10 droning through the night he came padding down the aisle on his stockinged feet to tell the travelling press, tucked in close to the tail with a seemingly immeasurable supply of buck's fizz and devils on horseback, of the gleams of hope perceptible amid the gloom.

Whatever gleams there were north of the South African border were rapidly extinguished by Kaunda, who kept the Foreign Secretary waiting for 15 minutes and then, more for the benefit of the media than for his guest, wondered aloud with much flicking of his white handkerchief and sorrowful rollings of his head whether Britain had sufficient moral responsibility to fight Nazism in South Africa. Kaunda, a son of the manse from Lubwa Mission and disciple of Gandhi, had evolved the state philosophy of Zambian Humanism – the 'good news about man' derived from the Bible, other writings and his own experience – as a protective solace against moods of despair induced by British duplicity and betrayal during the days of Rhodesian UDI. 'It is intended to be an antidote to corrosive cynicism, a tonic for drooping spirits – those appalled by the dark side of human nature', he has written.[2]

By the time Howe made a second trip (a fortnight later, during the course of his visit to Pretoria) corrosive cynicism was getting the upper hand and the Foreign Secretary, delegate from the dark side, sat hunched behind a bowl of lilies as Kaunda, after the customary 15-minute delay, delivered a bitter harangue before the media. Howe was not welcome as a messenger from Pretoria and he and Thatcher were involved in a conspiracy with Botha to maintain white rule. A lesser man would have walked out, but Howe sat it out and responded as best he could. This, he must have known by now, was the way African Commonwealth leaders of the old school tended to behave, a rambling series of insults delivered with impressive indifference to the manicured diplomatic processes of the West. The sad truth was that Howe was hardly a messenger since there was no new message worth speaking of from Pretoria. The raids which marked the end of the EPG mission had to be accepted as the only message available for the time being. Among the Front Line States Howe visited the only warm welcome came from President Machel of Mozambique who hoped, unavailingly, that a way would be found for his country to enter the Commonwealth, since it would bring him closer to a Britain he saw as protector and helper. As he flew home with a gift of prawns from Machel, about the only commodity his impoverished country had to give, Howe may well have reflected that relations with African countries outside the Commonwealth were considerably easier than with those inside. Apart from anything else, the latter were now wrecking the Commonwealth Games in Edinburgh with an organized boycott in protest at British policy.

Howe's mission ended in Pretoria on 29 July with a

meeting with President Botha. Sir Herbert Baker's pre-Delhi exercise in late imperial architecture, the Union Building on the hillside at Meintjeskop, provided a majestic forum for the President to state that a personal desire to stay alive politically was the reason why he was sending home the emissary of South Africa's former ruler empty-handed. 'I can never commit suicide by accepting threats and prescriptions from outside forces and hand South Africa over to communist forces in disguise.'

While Sir Geoffrey was busy with South Africa, a usually silent player emerged on the scene. Alarm was growing in Buckingham Palace that the Prime Minister's no-nonsense methods would before long send the Commonwealth down the same road as the Holy Roman Empire (to which, some savants thought, it bore a distinct resemblance) taking with it a considerable part of the monarchy's *raison d'être*. 'Sources close to the Queen' were quoted in *The Sunday Times* as saying that Thatcher's handling of the sanctions issue had caused royal displeasure. The Queen wanted a compromise on sanctions. The report was denounced by the Palace spokesman, as it was bound to be, but it had a ring of authenticity. The spirit of the views attributed to the Queen bore a resemblance to remarks made in April by the Prince of Wales when he and Mulroney jointly opened the Canadian pavilion at Expo '86 in Vancouver. 'I really do see the Commonwealth as a family. It has always been the role of the Crown to act as a unifying force, to emphasise the things we have in common rather than our differences.'

The mini-summit débâcle

The timing of the intervention appeared to be linked with the mini-summit, due to begin on 2 August, a few days after Howe returned from Pretoria. Statements out of Ottawa bore warnings, too. Mulroney's pre-summit envoy to the capitals of the Seven, Bernard Wood, head of the North-South Institute, reported the possibility that some countries would withdraw from the Commonwealth if Thatcher insisted on opposing sanctions. It would be 'absolutely disastrous' if when the mini-summit met in London she once again moved only a 'teensy-weensy' bit. Mulroney himself, as he boarded his plane for London, boldly insisted – if in rather opaque language – that Thatcher would have to accommodate herself 'to certain realities. One of them is Britain's membership of the Commonwealth, where we clearly stated (at Nassau) that ... we would get together and consider further measures.'

The patching up which occurred at the 1971 Singapore summit when Thatcher's Conservative predecessor Edward Heath, in the interests of Commonwealth unity, retreated at least part of the way from his government's decision to sell arms to South Africa did not take place this time. Mrs Thatcher was quite unmoved and the mini-summit marked the end of consensus as the main rule of the club. The founder member put it in writing, in a dissenting paragraph inserted in the final communiqué, that its policy on South Africa was made in the European Community, not in the Commonwealth. It would impose voluntary bans on new investment and the promotion of tourism, but sanctions on the import of coal, iron, steel and gold coins would have to wait on EC decisions. The six other leaders at the summit abided by the Nassau agreement and imposed the held-over part of the Nassau list (bans on air links, new investment, agricultural imports and other measures) plus bans on new bank loans, and the import of uranium, coal, iron and steel and the restriction of their consular facilities in South Africa to their own nationals and those of third countries for which they acted. Britain was isolated within the Commonwealth, and in terms of British prosperity and security that mattered not at all.

The break-up of the summit was predictably bitter. Kaunda accused Mrs Thatcher of worshipping gold and platinum and warned of possible economic reprisals, although he wisely did not spell out what measures were available to his near-bankrupt state. She had cut a 'very pathetic figure' at the summit. The Zambian President's neighbour Mugabe declared that 'Britain has failed us' and that Mrs Thatcher was an ally of apartheid. In Hawke's view, the Commonwealth had been offered a choice between unity and credibility and had chosen the latter. Gandhi sensed betrayal: Britain stood accused of compromising the 'noble parts' of its history and was no longer the Commonwealth's leader. And Mulroney grandly gave it as his opinion that Thatcher's refusal to heed his 'straightforward' urgings to endorse action consistent with human liberty and human rights would be judged not by him, but by the British people.

Britain, said Canada's only national newspaper, *The Globe and Mail* of Toronto, had become a 'virtual pariah state'. Expulsion from the Commonwealth would have been likely except that a Commonwealth without Britain was inconceivable and it was hard to envisage a rump organization with headquarters in Ottawa (which, some were muttering, was what might happen). And then came an interesting recognition of a sort not often publicly expressed in Canada, that the South African issue might have got out of hand.[3]

If British influence and commitment to the institution is in decline, does that mean the sun is destined to set on the four corners of the Commonwealth? That will be its fate if the Africans continue to treat it as a one-issue coalition whose members are to be mobilised by threats of break-up. Even a Canadian leader as sympathetic to African aspirations as Brian Mulroney can hardly be enamoured by the blackmail tactics employed by Zambian President Kenneth Kaunda. It would be a sorry spectacle if the Commonwealth were to become a hopelessly polarised and therefore paralysed forum. Its demise would then be inevitable. And while such an outcome would not be apocalyptic, it would deprive the world of a useful set of undertakings in the areas of development and technical assistance, athletic, educational and cultural exchanges.

In mid-September the European Community foreign ministers agreed a sanctions package, rather weaker than the one proposed at the June summit, but estimated to cut South African exports to the EC by $575m. Howe announced British implementation when he spoke to the UN General Assembly on 25 September. A Foreign Office statement called the sanctions 'a legitimate and necessary political signal to the South African government' and reiterated the familiar – and in most Commonwealth eyes, highly suspect – position that they were limited and specific in order to avoid 'further destabilisation of the South African economy and harming those in South Africa whom we are seeking to help'. On 30 September Howe delivered a speech entitled 'The Commonwealth: Who Cares?' to the Commonwealth Parliamentary Conference in London. Of course South Africa was of vital concern to the Commonwealth, he said with a placatory nod to the Africans in the audience, but it needed to be kept in perspective. There was more to Africa than just the problems of one of its countries. The rest of Africa should think more about their economic problems. Help could come from the Commonwealth which was 'well suited to this practical, sensible work'. It was an organization which passed the test of relevance and effectiveness and its ministerial meetings 'generally' concentrated on 'practical exchanges of views and realistic joint commitments'. The meetings must not be devalued; the forum was too precious to waste.

The image summoned up by Howe was that of a 'caring Commonwealth' (his phrase) which included a caring Britain, generous with its aid. By the time the October 1987 summit in Vancouver came round a policy for Southern Africa had been elaborated ready for presentation in a neat booklet with maps, graphs and illustrations.[4] The emphasis was on aid and development and the approach treated Southern Africa as a regional problem which included Mozambique and Angola as well as Commonwealth countries and South Africa and Namibia. The collective organization for the black countries concerned was not the Commonwealth but the Southern African Development Co-ordination Conference (SADCC), which has its headquarters in Gaborone, the Botswana capital.[5] The British aims were set out as follows:

* to work for peaceful dialogue in South Africa leading to the elimination of apartheid and its replacement by a non-racial representative system of government
* to help promote the peaceful, stable and prosperous development of all States in the region.

These two aims are inextricably linked – only through the abolition of apartheid will South Africa be able to forge stable, friendly relations with her neighbours.

A 'non-racial representative government' did not, of course, mean black majority rule or one-man-one-vote. It was also a policy which left open the possibility of investment and aid for a South Africa which moved towards the required goal, as Mrs Thatcher was to suggest during the summit. The SADCC countries would be helped to become more self-sufficient, thus reducing their dependence on South Africa, which maintains a grip on railways and ports vital to most of them. Since change in South Africa could only come from within, there would be help in training and educating blacks who would prepare the way for a 'successful post-apartheid society', which could – according to the glosses added by British officials – be 15 years or more away. The figures for British aid to SADCC countries in 1980–86 were impressive: a total of £819m.

Vancouver

The Vancouver summit was held in the trade and conference centre, a bulky piece of fun-architecture which crossed the motifs of cruise liner, warehouse and sailing ship on a pier facing across a massive harbour whose autumnal placidity was broken by the wakes of ferries and the comings and goings of sea-planes. The Thatcher policy on South Africa was at least consistent and when her turn came to speak, there can have been few among her fellow heads of government who did not know it by heart. There was nothing to be gained by parading their differences, she told them. 'What we do all agree is that apartheid is an utterly repulsive and detestable system and it must go. So it would be much better if the message which goes out from our meeting is one of agreement on positive action.'

The British line, as promoted by Bernard Ingham, the Downing Street spokesman, was that sanctions were 'off the boil', and some support for this view came from Joe Clark, the Canadian External Affairs Minister. In July he had told the UN that 'there must be no relenting in that campaign, no pause in the pressure', but he now admitted that 'temporary sanctions fatigue' appeared to have set in. Kaunda, who was current chairman of the Front Line States and the Organization of African Unity, omitted the word sanctions from his speech. Mugabe, then chairman of the Non-Aligned Movement, was humiliatingly aware when he spoke at the opening of the summit that he had had to back away from the sanctions agreed at Nassau and London and that the Non-Aligned summit in Harare in September 1986 had provided nothing more substantial than moral support. The Zimbabwe tobacco crop was still shipped through South Africa and flights between Johannesburg and Harare went on as if no one had heard of sanctions. The Australian press coverage of the conference concentrated on Fiji almost to the exclusion of South Africa. Even in Canada there was a gap between promise and performance. The severance of diplomatic relations with South Africa was not in prospect despite Mulroney's undertakings on that score before the UN General Assembly in 1985 and there had been no delay in the acceptance of the credentials of a new South African ambassador to Ottawa in 1987. Nevertheless, Ramphal firmly denied in an eve-of-summit speech to a meeting organized by anti-apartheid campaigners that sanctions were 'off the boil'. The Commonwealth had to build on them and strengthen them.

Mulroney's political stock was at a low point during the summit. His Conservative Party was wiped out to the last man in the New Brunswick provincial election and there were reports that officials of the External Affairs Ministry had taken to drawing the attention of visiting journalists to opinion polls showing waning support for his South African policy.[6] He was portrayed by the same officials as having broken ranks with the US, British and other West European governments by abandoning a 25-year-old policy under which the evils of apartheid were denounced but otherwise it was business as usual provided there was some evidence of reform. Mulroney felt obliged to say two days before the summit that 'There shouldn't be any doubt in the minds of anyone, External or otherwise, what the policy is'.

The British had had no love for Mulroney since the Nassau summit. He was clearly not Mrs Thatcher's type of Conservative, merely a crypto-liberal intent on showing off his good intentions before an audience which knew little of what was happening in the world outside its sub-arctic domain. His remarks after the mini-summit about leaving judgment on Thatcher to the British people still rankled. His political weakness was seen as an opportunity for vengeance and a Canadian proposal for a foreign ministers' committee to monitor the effectiveness of sanctions and make recommendations for increasing pressure on South Africa was instantly and patronizingly dismissed by the British as being of 'somewhat uncertain purpose' and likely to drive Botha in the wrong direction.

This was followed by a botched mugging in which the instrument was the British media briefing. Ingham produced International Monetary Fund figures which showed that Canadian exports to South Africa had risen by 47 per cent in 1985–6. There was no arguing with the figures; they were undoubtedly correct. What smacked of dirty tricks was the way in which the British had drawn attention to them, and the fact that they were out of date. Mulroney denounced Thatcher for spreading nonsense and being impolite. He countered with figures which demonstrated that exports for the first eight months of 1987 showed a 50 per cent drop compared with the same period in 1986; the rise in the IMF figures was the result of a one-off sale of aircraft. A cry went up from the frustrated assembly in Vancouver that the British had made a wicked attempt to malign a decent right-minded host. A remarkable press conference was convened at the end of the summit at which Hawke, Gandhi, Kaunda and Mugabe announced their joint support for the unjustly accused Mulroney and denounced the 'disinformation and misinformation' disseminated at British briefings. Hawke accused British newspapers of spreading an 'abominably untrue statement'.[7] Mugabe professed himself to be 'completely disillusioned and in a way dismayed' by British dishonesty. And Gandhi likened Thatcher's attitude to Botha to Neville Chamberlain's appeasement of Hitler; the rest of the Commonwealth were like Winston Churchill who knew evil had to be faced and fought.

The Canadians may have emerged shining white in Vancouver, but they were not so fortunate nearly 15 months later when their sincerity was once again questioned. In February 1989 Foreign Minister Clark was obliged, while chairing a meeting on sanctions in Zimbabwe, to admit that Canadian exports to South Africa had risen by 44 per cent in 1988 and imports by 66 per cent. Canada's commitment to the sanctions battle looked even more like a sanctimonious front to 'business as usual' in commercial quarters when news arrived at the same conference that the Canadian Government had sanctioned a £250m. loan by the Bank of Nova Scotia to the South African-owned Minorco company to help it buy Consolidated Goldfields. Allan Boesak, the coloured South African anti-apartheid leader, called the loan a 'vast betrayal' of South Africa's blacks.[8]

The Okanagan Statement and Programme of Action on Southern Africa, produced in a British Columbian resort to which the Vancouver summit retreated for two days, was another non-consensus document. It included five dissents by Britain from the conclusions on sanctions and one from the summit's decision to set up a committee of eight foreign ministers to provide 'impetus and guidance' on sanctions and other measures. Mulroney found comfort in the Commonwealth's leadership in the sanctions struggle. 'We came here in an atmosphere in which sanctions were to be set aside . . . but we have reaffirmed our commitment.'

Britain was being cast off, left to its own curmudgeonly devices. There was an element in all this of the story of Sam Goldwyn leaning over the stern rail of the *Queen Mary* shouting 'Bon Voyage' at the receding skyline of New York. It was, after all, Britain which was staying put, concentrating on its own interests. The Canadians were at the helm of the foreign ministers committee and none too sure where they would sail it; and indeed its course was to prove wavering and uncertain as they moderated their enthusiasm for sanctions in an attempt to find ways of ensuring that Britain was among the welcoming party when everyone came ashore for the Kuala Lumpur summit in 1989.

The Canadians have tried to put a brave face on Vancouver, but it was a forlorn occasion. The Queen lost the Crown of Fiji there when her Governor-General, Ratu Sir Penaia Ganilau, resigned and Fiji's membership of the Commonwealth was deemed to have lapsed until the time came, if it ever did, when its constitutional and racial problems were resolved. Vancouver was notable, too, for Thatcher's disclosure of what she really thought about the ANC, the EPG's chief candidate for dialogue with Botha: 'a typical terrorist organization'.

The party was over so far as Africa was concerned. Thatcher had demonstrated two things quite conclusively: Britain was not assuming responsibility for 'decolonization' in South Africa, and the Commonwealth had no levers, moral, political or economic, which could bend Britain's policies towards a consensus policy which its government believed would be damaging to British economic interests. Attached to that position was the rider that sanctions aimed at collapsing the South African economy would be beneficial to none of the country's inhabitants. Majority rule was not, in British eyes, a desirable goal. The British had plumped for power sharing; their approach would be gradualist and aimed at ensuring that the sharing would be equitable, but the timetable could extend over many years, well outside Thatcher's tenure of office. Those who demanded comprehensive sanctions might attack what they saw as a blatant example of British hypocrisy, but there was no avoiding another factor in a situation which had greatly changed since the 1970s and the Rhodesia crisis. British foreign policy was becoming more and more integrated with that of the European Community. The consensus on South Africa would be made in Brussels. In the last resort, the Commonwealth was expendable so far as the British were concerned.

7
The Politics of Aid

THERE WAS one question left hanging in the still October air as the presidents and prime ministers left Vancouver in October 1987. Why had no one handed in his membership card and announced his resignation from the club? If one took African demands at their face value, the campaign for comprehensive sanctions had, quite clearly, been a monstrous failure. Three summits had come and gone and the measures which would supposedly starve white South Africa into submission were as elusive as ever. Within the terms of the definitions offered by the African political lexicon, Mrs Thatcher was definitely a racist and, therefore, the Commonwealth was, by association, fatally infected by the same virus. Yet there they all were, without defections, shaking hands as they departed and telling one another how much they looked forward to meeting again in two years' time in Kuala Lumpur.

The answer to the question is that the Commonwealth is rather more than a forum in which moral indignation can be let loose on post-colonial guilt. It is, among other things, a framework on which the two richest members hang their aid packages, the lion's share of which are labelled 'Africa'. Britain accounts for 34 per cent of the Commonwealth's total GNP, Canada for 24 per cent. If you are the leader of a country like Zambia, where per capita income is less than £250 a year and GNP is shrinking rather than increasing, you think twice before impetuously announcing a resignation which might seriously imperil relations with your most consistent aid donor who is also a member of the Group of Seven, the leading Western industrial nations, and a power among the multilateral aid and financial organizations. Not, of course, that that stopped Kenneth Kaunda from being impolite to Sir Geoffrey Howe in mid-1986, but that was before maize price riots set him on a course which was to lead in May 1987 to the termination of a series of austerity agreements with the International Monetary Fund. He had had enough of 'structural adjustment', the buzz-phrase euphemism in international aid circles for obliging pauper nations to live within their means. He announced rather grandly later on that 'co-operation must be on the basis of equality because, big or small, each one of us is endowed with the same soul from God Almighty and as such we want equality in all that we think, say and do'.[1] Kaunda did not resign from the IMF, either. By the end of 1987 he was running out of friends and in a more temperate frame of mind. The reprisal for his treatment of Sir Geoffrey was delayed until November 1988 when Downing Street let it be known that Lusaka had been left off the list of African capitals Thatcher planned to visit in April 1989. But at least it was chastisement within the club. Feelings were hurt, Kaunda's role as the elder statesman of the Front Line States had been diminished, but the damage was not irreparable.

The summits of 1985-7 coincided with a heightened international awareness of the direness of Africa's predicament: civil wars, famine, AIDS and statistical projections of huge increases in population which only famine and disease were likely to stop. South Africa ranked low in the list of catastrophes, probably lower in most African perceptions than locusts. Of the 87 disasters to which Britain responded with official help in 1987, 56 were in African countries south of the Mediterranean fringe of Arab states. The UN Special Session on Africa in June 1986 adopted a five-year programme which basically committed the Africans to greater efforts to put their barebones economies in order in return for more help from the developed world. According to the World Bank, Africa's terms of trade deteriorated by 32 per cent in that year and the purchasing power of its exports, almost all primary commodities, fell by between 26 and 30 per cent.

Servicing debts swallowed a further 30 per cent of the reduced earnings; and in September 1988 a UN review conference heard that since the start of the five-year recovery programme per capita income had dropped a further 4 per cent. Despite harder efforts Sub-Saharan Africa was still $2 billion a year short of the aid and debt relief it needed to swim rather than merely keep its head above water.

The fact that 70 per cent of Britain's bilateral aid goes to Commonwealth countries underlines the continuing importance to Britain of the Commonwealth, even if its multilateral aspects, such as the Secretariat, are of diminishing significance. Concentration on the Commonwealth undoubtedly makes the aid programme more effective in political and practical terms than if it were more widely dispersed. However, Britain is a miser among aid donors and its record since the Conservatives came to power in 1979 illustrates a flinty reappraisal which has downgraded the Third World in the course of reshuffling the priorities competing for a share of resources. In 1979 aid as a percentage of GNP amounted to 0.51; in 1987 the percentage was 0.28. If one adjusts gross public expenditure on aid to 1987 prices, it has fallen from the equivalent of £1,704m. in 1979 to £1,271m. in 1987.[2] In 1987 Britain was fourteenth in the Organization for Economic Co-operation and Development's list of the 18 major aid donors, whose average is 0.34 per cent of GNP. Since then, realization of the extent of the Third World's problems has reversed the downward trend, but in real terms the aid programme will still be running well below the 1979 level even in 1991–2.

Aid is given for a variety of reasons which include compassion and goodwill. The donor's ability to withdraw his goodwill can cause a recipient to hesitate before testing it too far. India is the largest single recipient of British (and European Community) aid, but a breakdown of the figures shows that 38 per cent of the British total goes to countries in the category 'Africa South of the Sahara'. This includes Ethiopia, Mozambique (a major recipient) and a wide spread of other non-Commonwealth countries, but the biggest beneficiaries are Commonwealth members led by Kenya (£28m. in 1987) followed by Malawi, Zambia and Tanzania.[3] It is easier to give aid to countries where officials speak

English and where there is a history of mutual knowledge. Ulterior motives such as leverage are, of course, always denied. Replying in October 1987 to a Foreign Affairs Select Committee report, the Foreign Office stated flatly that: 'The business of the aid programme is aid' and there were no separate developmental, commercial or political objectives.[4]

There is one objective, which is the promotion of development. This is entirely compatible with also serving our political, industrial and commercial interests. Development has many faces, among them social, humanitarian, political and commercial. Higher living standards are likely to create stable, thriving and solvent trading partners. Development is concerned with sustainable, long-term benefits rather than short-term ones; with political stability rather than short-term popularity; with the development of markets rather than the securing of an order.

Which is high-minded and diffuse in the best tradition of the British foreign service. In fact, commercial objectives have a high ranking among objectives. The amount of British aid tied to the provision of British goods and services is almost twice the average among the 18 countries on the OECD list, a fact which has caused concern to the OECD's Development Assistance Committee and the UK Foreign Affairs Select Committee.[5] Only Italy and Austria tie a higher proportion.

As for aid's political objectives, Southern Africa is an excellent example of how important they are. British policy, as it emerged at Vancouver from the lips of Mrs Thatcher, is best seen as an attempt to treat the region as one big running sore. There is a moral distinction caused by apartheid, but it is obscured by the stated belief that, given time, market and demographic forces will erode the boundaries between the races. Thus, the cure for apartheid is the strengthening of the modern economy and a steady increase in the numbers participating in it. The countries immediately to the north of South Africa (or, in the case of Lesotho, actually within it) cannot cut themselves off, but they can loosen Pretoria's grip by improving their economies and their communications infrastructure. Restoring the railway network has meant helping Mozambique (which until the mid-1970s used to earn

70 per cent of its foreign exchange from transit traffic) and its neighbours defeat Renamo, the faceless, ostensibly anti-marxist organization which has had South African military backing. British instructors are training Mozambican units in Zimbabwe and nearly £3m. has been spent on providing 'non-lethal' equipment (mainly Land-Rovers, trucks and radios) for the armies of Mozambique, Tanzania (which withdrew from northern Mozambique at the end of 1988), Malawi and Zimbabwe. These forces guard three vital railway lines, all linking the interior with the Indian Ocean: the Nacala line from Malawi across northern Mozambique; the Beira corridor (which includes a road and an oil pipeline), and the Limpopo railway, which links Zimbabwe with Maputo. Britain is participating in the rehabilitation of all three lines.

The Commonwealth may not be the anvil on which British policies are forged, but it is still a pressure group which has helped keep alive Britain's commitment to the welfare and survival of the Front Line States. British support for the SADCC (Southern African Development Co-ordination Conference) states has made it more difficult for South Africa to continue with an active destabilization policy aimed at keeping its neighbours dependent on South African railways and ports. Contrary to the impression which its leadership often gives, South Africa is not a country immune to international opinion. It may have no friends other than Israel and Taiwan but, as an industrialized nation, it is aware of the need not to push the leading members of the industrialized world, particularly Britain, the United States and West Germany, into a situation where public outrage obliges their governments to lift their limited protection and end their trade.

By the beginning of 1989 there were signs that international tensions in the Southern African region as a whole were easing. Economically and militarily, there were powerful incentives for South Africa to end its entanglement in Angola and agree to UN-supervised elections which would create an independent Namibia. Combined with President Gorbachev's desire to rid the Soviet Union of politically and financially expensive foreign commitments such as the Cuban military presence in Angola, they provided an opening for an

American-mediated tripartite agreement linking Cuban and South African withdrawals to free elections and independence in Namibia. After almost a decade of frustration, the US policy of 'constructive engagement' with South Africa could record a success. President Botha's visit to Mozambique in autumn 1988 indicated that destabilization in the form of aid to Renamo had indeed come to an end. Within South Africa the picture was mixed: further restrictions on the press and right-wing Conservative victories in local elections set against the transfer of Mandela from prison to house arrest and the commutation of the death sentences on the Sharpeville Six. However, the central issue of African political rights had still to be addressed.

The EC context

Some 42 per cent of Britain's 1987 aid was channelled through multilateral agencies, almost wholly European Community and United Nations. At the back of the Overseas Development Administration's 1987 review, in the section entitled 'Special Articles', pride of place is given to the thoughts of Christopher Patten, Minister for Overseas Development, on how to improve European Community aid. The article is based on a speech given at the Royal Commonwealth Society in May 1988, and its relevance to the Commonwealth lies chiefly in the fact that exactly half the 66 ACP (Africa, Caribbean and Pacific) states covered by the Lomé Conventions governing trade and aid relations between the Community and the poorest and smallest ex-colonies are members of the Commonwealth. The Lomé Convention, signed in 1975 following Britain's entry into the EC in 1973, drew a line under the remaining imperial preferences, thereby at the same time ending what remained of the Commonwealth's economic *raison d'être*.

Looked at from a different perspective, however, British entry opened up new opportunities for many of the poor Commonwealth countries. Through Britain they were linked with the largest collective source of aid and (Patten's phrase) 'the most generous trading system in the modern world'.

Lomé Conventions run in five-year spans and negotiations on Lomé IV began in mid-October 1988, with March 1990 as the date when it would come into effect. The 'areas of importance' Patten mentioned as deserving examination in a 'sympathetic and positive spirit' reflect Commonwealth interest in maintaining special trade arrangements for sugar, bananas, beef and rum. Sugar is of primary importance to Mauritius, Guyana, Jamaica, Swaziland, Barbados, Kenya, Malawi, Tanzania, Trinidad and Uganda (and Fiji, too, where it is by a large margin the main export). Beef affects Botswana, Zimbabwe, Kenya and Swaziland. Rum and bananas are of concern to all Commonwealth Caribbean countries. What the ACP countries also want – and will argue for in the Lomé IV negotiations – is help with setting up manufacturing industries and access for their products.

Sixty per cent of the Community's Third World aid goes to the ACP countries, whose main bonus from Lomé is duty-free access to Community markets for all but a minute fraction of their products. But the distinctiveness of even this huge ex-colonial section of the world is threatened as other small developing countries clamour for inclusion. The Community attitude is by no means based on selflessness. The Third World is, in bloc terms, the Community's biggest customer, taking 34 per cent of its exports, mainly manufactured goods, in 1985.[6]

The Commonwealth Secretariat played an active part, through Ramphal, in the negotiation of the first Lomé Convention and its involvement continues in the negotiation of the fourth. (It has paid the fees of two experts employed to draw up memoranda for the ACP countries and has commissioned several studies.) The Secretariat has no right of representation within the negotiations, however, and the Commonwealth countries look to Britain to champion their cause. This they did with rather more confidence as the negotiations for Lomé IV opened than had been the case with Lomé III, when it was felt that the French had been much more active and successful in obtaining a good deal for their ex-colonies. The Francophone countries seem to have considerably more cohesion within the ACP than Commonwealth countries. The latter tend not to collaborate to concert a joint position but to work within regional groupings. 'Everyone speaks English these days', explained an official from one of the Commonwealth Caribbean islands, 'and the French-speaking ACP countries tend to feel a bit beleaguered, so they stick together. France keeps a close grip on them, too.'

The case of Canada

Canada is a country without colonial responsibilities past or present, but despite that good fortune it has enthusiastically accepted the obligations of the British Empire as part of its inheritance and insists on sharing those of France, despite some French misgivings. The Canadian commentator and journalist, Richard Gwyn, in his examination of US-Canadian relations, *The 49th Paradox*,[7] quotes the poet Douglas LePan's description of Canada as 'a country without a mythology'. This is not quite true; there is, after all, the ice-bound north and the saga of the long and troubled search for a joint nationhood of British and French. But there is enough truth in it for Gwyn to make his point that the idealistic aspects of Canada's foreign policy are partly an attempt to compensate. This is Canada as it likes to see itself: outward-looking, generous, a touch Scandinavian in its compassionate approach to the Third World, and entirely different in this respect from its southern neighbour. Canada gave 0.45 per cent of its GNP in aid in 1987 (in cash terms, about the same amount as Britain), while the United States gave a mere 0.20 per cent, the same as Ireland but a bit more than Austria. Aid began for Canada in the 1950s with the Colombo Plan[8] (originally a Commonwealth organization and still listed as such) and was concentrated at that time almost entirely on Asian Commonwealth countries. Since then much has changed. The Commonwealth and *La Francophonie* are useful as assemblages through which to express benevolence; and they have the added advantage that the United States cannot belong to them. Lester Pearson in his memoirs (notes Gwyn) states that Canada uses international institutions 'to escape the danger of a too-exclusively continental relationship (with the United States), without forfeiting the political and economic advantages of that inevitable and vitally important relationship'. Canada's is clearly a fairly uneasy independence, given US domination of its economy, trade and culture, and the 1988 Free Trade Agreement (labelled by the Liberals as the 'Sale of Canada Act') seems likely in the long term to reduce it to a condition of economic autonomy not much more pronounced than that of the Isle of Man in its relations with the United Kingdom. Aid as an expression of national identity will thus become even more important.

Canadian aid is administered through the Canadian International Development Agency, created some twenty years ago at the start of the Trudeau era. Like British aid, it is focused heavily on Africa. 'Africa remained at the heart of our considerations', wrote Mme Monique Landry, the Minister responsible for CIDA, in the 1986–7 annual review. Africa, including the Arab countries of the north, took over 43 per cent of Canada's bilateral aid in that year. There is a sizeable constituency for aid in Canada (which there is not in Britain or the United States), but there is an additional motive governing the way in which aid is divided between Anglophone and Francophone countries. Canada, it has been said, suffers from two permanent crises: one is its relations with the United States, the other the internal relationship between English-speaking and French-speaking Canadians. The pattern of the distribution of aid to Africa can be seen as an aspect of the latter. Both groups get almost equal amounts. The only anomaly is Anglophone Tanzania, the biggest recipient today – over a third more than any other country – as it was at the beginning of the 1970s, a tribute to the alluring if generally misguided policies of that persuasive Commonwealth statesman, Julius Nyerere.

Canadian foreign ministers have tended to take a more sceptical view of the Commonwealth than their prime ministers. Mitchell Sharp thought the cursory reference to it in his department's 1970 foreign policy review reflected the 'reality of the world'. It was not a policy-making body or a trade promotion organization; 'It's a place where we can meet with countries with some sort of common links with the past'.[9] Trudeau, by contrast, had come back from his first Commonwealth summit, in London in 1969, a convert. The

Commonwealth, he had discovered, was 'an organism, not an institution'. It had flexibility and promised continued growth and vitality. Just as importantly, perhaps, the 1960s political flower child had, like other Canadian prime ministers, been impressed by the summit's potential as a stage. A Canadian leader cut an important figure on it; he held the centre and could act usefully as a mediator, and there was domestic support for this role. His predecessor Pearson had occupied this position and Trudeau did the same at Singapore in 1971. Peter Dobell wrote of the Singapore summit,[10]

The government, probably to its surprise, found itself being pressed on the domestic front to affirm that it would not withdraw [from the Commonwealth], no matter whether some of the African States were to do so, and was even urged to step into Britain's place if Britain withdrew. No obvious explanation emerged for this interest, but it was widespread and genuine enough to persuade the government that vigorous efforts to save the Commonwealth would avoid the more difficult choices to be made if it disappeared.

None of the initiatives his government had undertaken since it was elected in 1968 had given him more pride than those which were Commonwealth-oriented, Trudeau was to say a year or two later.[11] But it was one of two threads in his policy towards the Third World. The other was his use of *La Francophonie* to 'spin a new fibre of unity within Canada'. *Francophonie* involved Quebec. It redressed Canada's overwhelming tilt towards the English-speaking world as represented by the Commonwealth and the United States; and aid programmes in its Third World countries provided jobs for French-speaking Canadians. Moreover, by participating in the founding conferences of *L'Agence de Coopération Culturelle et Technique* (ACCT) in Niamey, the capital of Niger, in 1969 and 1970, and providing a third of the start-up costs, Canada thwarted French plans to recognize Quebec as an independent member. The first regular meetings of ACCT were held in Ottawa and Quebec in October 1971 and Quebec was admitted as a 'participating government', separate from the list of member countries. Since then New Brunswick, which has a sizeable minority of French-speakers, has joined in the same category.

La Francophonie

The Francophone movement is, in fact, a pretty broad church. Luxembourg, Switzerland, Belgium and its former colonies Zaire, Rwanda and Burundi are among the members. Egypt attended the first Francophone summit in Paris in 1986, so, too, did Morocco and Tunisia. No Arab country, not even Sudan, has ever belonged to the Commonwealth, but the easier political terms presented by a linguistic and cultural union make it possible for them to participate in *La Francophonie*. The structures created by France around the use of the French language are simple compared with the Commonwealth, and they have not so far become overtly politicized. France provides between three and four times as much aid as Britain and is seen as an effective promoter of African interests in the European Community, so it is not surprising that its Franco-African summits – instituted in the 1970s – draw in countries from outside the French cultural community. The close ties with its former colonies are maintained by a pre-summit caucus. The Francophone summits have so far shied away from turning the ACCT into a secretariat, even though its importance in implementing their conclusions has been acknowledged. Instead, there is a Paris-based organizing committee, chaired in 1987–8 by the Canadian ambassador in Paris. At the second Francophone summit, held in Quebec in September 1987, a month before the Commonwealth met in Vancouver, President Mitterrand's outline of the principal areas on which the participants should concentrate their thoughts in advance of the next summit sounded like Mrs Thatcher's dream agenda for the Commonwealth: agriculture, energy, culture and communication, technical and scientific information and language sciences. There was even agreement on a flag for *La Francophonie*, a circle composed of red, blue, yellow, green and violet parts, symbolizing the five continents, on a white background. A slight note of disharmony was noted when, shortly before the Quebec summit, Canada doubled its contribution to ACCT; *Le Monde* commented gravely that Canada had 'tossed a rock into the garden of the French'.

The prescription laid down by Mitterrand for the agenda of the next summit was, in fact, remarkably similar to the objectives contained in article 1 of the ACCT's charter adopted in 1970. It stipulated multilateral co-operation in education, culture, science and technology as the 'essential aim' of the agency.

It works in absolute respect for the sovereignty of states, languages and cultures, and observes the strictest neutrality in matters of an ideological and political nature. It collaborates with the various international and regional organizations and takes account of all the forms of existing technical and cultural co-operation.

How do the French, unlike the British, manage to escape without becoming politically embroiled? One answer is that the ACCT was founded well after the end of the Vietnamese and Algerian conflicts. By contrast, the Commonwealth Secretariat was born out of the clash between Britain and the newly independent African colonies over Rhodesia. A report[12] on the ratification of the agreement establishing the ACCT which was presented to the French National Assembly in June 1970 noted several factors which were present at the creation of *La Francophonie*: decolonization, reaction to the 'cultural influence of the English-speaking world' and the end of the Algerian war. Curiously, though, the 'decisive year' for both organizations was 1965 and the impetus came from Africa, in the case of *Francophonie* from President Senghor of Senegal, the poet and philosopher of *Négritude*, a West African like Nkrumah, the proposer of the Commonwealth Secretariat. Senghor's proposal had similarities with the Commonwealth (and may well have been shaped by what was happening in London) to the extent that it created a forum for the ex-colonial power and its former colonies: a general secretariat, periodic meetings of ministers, particularly finance ministers, and an emphasis on the economic solidarity of industrialized and non-industrialized French-speaking countries. It coincided with the French government's decision to set up the High Committee for the Defence and Spread of the French Language. Where Senghor differed from Nkrumah was in his fundamental concept. Nkrumah was all politics and liberation; Senghor's idea was born in a bower of cultural harmony. *Négritude's* companion was *Francité*, being part of the spirit of French civilization and culture. France had provided 'the leaven to bring ancient exotic civilizations back to life by the grafting of the French branch. France has enabled the Arabs to be more Arab, the Negroes to be more Negro.'

Anglophile maharajahs may have said things like that once upon a time, but it is hard to think of any post-war leader from the African Commonwealth extolling the spirit of British culture as the reason for unity. Charles Njonjo, the suave and immaculately suited former Kenyan Attorney-General, known mockingly in Nairobi as the Duke of Kabetshire, was, in the years before his political downfall in 1984, the nearest thing Anglophone Africa has produced to a French African politician. British Africans were not on the whole urged to bathe themselves in the mystique of high culture, adopting in the process the manners and tailoring of the metropolis.

It would, of course, have been impossible to have had an Anglophone movement in place of, or as a companion to, the Commonwealth. It would have been swamped by the Americans, who are an Anglophone movement all of their own. And it would have been difficult to know where to draw the line. Would the Israelis and South Africans be excluded from an apolitical organization founded on cultural affinities?

Nevertheless, regardless of the differences, there is an increasing fuzziness around the edges of these movements born out of empires (the Spanish and Portuguese have begun to form theirs, too, now that they are inside the European Community). The Quebec Francophone summit was hosted by a bilingual 'Quebec Anglo', Brian Mulroney, 'the Boy from Baie-Comeau', Prime Minister of a Queen who is also Head of the Commonwealth. Non-French-speaking countries can take part in the Franco-African summits; Mozambique has become an honorary member of the Commonwealth. A good example of the same process can be seen in the Commonwealth Development Corporation, a British public corporation under the thumb of the Foreign and Commonwealth Office and funded by government loans which it repays with interest. It invests long-term in projects and is a part-owner of some of them, providing management and other support services. Provided it has ministerial approval, it is allowed to invest outside the Commonwealth and has done so in eleven countries.

A similar catholicity is shown by the Crown Agents whose board is appointed by the Foreign Secretary and which administers more than £2 billion in loans and grants for aid organizations, chiefly the Overseas Development Administration, and in addition can look after purchases (from any source), shipping and insurance and financial advice among other things. Most of the clients and the projects it administers are Commonwealth or closely associated with Britain, but it has extended to a number of countries outside the circle, such as China, Mexico and Indonesia. It has offices in, among other places, South Korea, Japan, Venezuela and the United States, and it is moving hesitantly towards privatization.

Or take, as the ultimate example of the increasingly global nature of aid programmes, Chris Patten's speech at Chatham House in October 1988 when he suggested that Britain should help the Japanese spend the $50 billion they are planning to hand out in the next five years. 'At its zenith, Japanese aid will be like the sun, at which most of the world's poorest countries will be able to warm their hands and in the glare of which other donors' aid may lose some colour,' he declared with a suitably oriental floweriness. Britain had a deep knowledge of many of the world's poorest countries, it was an acknowledged master at ensuring that aid was well spent and qualitatively good, and it could act as guide and, quite literally, interpreter for the Japanese as they moved into lands previously trodden only by Honda and Hitachi salesmen. Work on co-operation had already started. He had been to Tokyo, had presented a programme of action afterwards, and hardly a week went by without the arrival of Japanese aid administrators and businessmen at the Overseas Development Administration. Perhaps no other speech in recent years has illustrated quite so clearly the changing attitude of

Britain towards its old empire. Ten or twenty years earlier the prospect of a deluge of aid from a nation remembered for overrunning the Eastern empire and associated in British minds with ruthless commercial rivalry would have been a matter for alarm and suspicion. In the new and increasingly unpossessive mood of 1988 it was being welcomed on behalf of a Commonwealth whose distinctiveness was increasingly becoming blurred by a wider internationalism.

8
The International Monarchy

THE OFFICIAL *Canada Handbook* included in the package of documents, maps and booklets handed to those arriving at the Vancouver summit was a standard production: a wrap-around photograph of maples in fall colours and a rocky stream on the cover, chapters inside on the environment, the people, industry, education, government and so on. Nothing unusual except for an omission. There was no picture of the Head of State, Queen Elizabeth II, at that moment beginning a tour of her realm. The chapter headed 'Government and Legal System' had obviously presented the compilers with some difficulties. It was topped with a picture of Prime Minister Mulroney and his family, seated grinning amiably on the stairway of the official residence in Ottawa. The facing page showed Governor-General Jeanne Sauvé and her husband leaving Parliament Hill, Ottawa, in an open landau amid a scene of red-coated military ceremony. Two pages later came the Queen Mother, in soft-focus black and white, celebrating her 85th birthday with her four grandchildren. The Queen did rather better in the text, which began with an acknowledgement that Canada was a constitutional monarchy. Nevertheless, the authors felt it necessary to distance themselves with inverted commas from a statement that executive government is vested in the Queen of Canada. From all this it may be gathered that the Queen has a somewhat ambiguous position in Canada. She is there constitutionally, but in the image presented to the world she is not allowed to upstage Prime Minister Mulroney or her official representative Governor-General Sauvé.

It was an aspect of the protracted row caused by the Quebec secessionists in the 1960s and 1970s that Pierre Trudeau promoted the role of the Governor-General (a Canadian nominated by the Prime Minister and then appointed by the Queen), sending him on state visits abroad. It was not only the Canadian Constitution which was 'patriated' in 1982, when the last rather theoretical vestiges of British authority were removed; so was the Head of State. For practical purposes, the Queen is Head of State only when she is in Canada. For the rest of the time her powers are exercised by the Governor-General.

Canada is the most frequently visited of the Queen's realms outside the United Kingdom, but not, according to some observers, her favourite. They claim she never seems as happy there as on her Antipodean trips. Perhaps memories linger of the rough ride she received from the Québecois in 1964 when she was booed in Quebec City and told to go home. Whatever the truth of that, no monarch wants to lose a crown through neglect and she visited Canada ten times between 1970 and 1988 (as compared with eight visits to Australia). It is a reasonable assumption, though, that Canada needs the Queen rather more than she needs it. The Queen, the Commonwealth and parliamentary government are the most substantial institutions Anglophone Canadians have to hang on to when it comes to establishing their national identity vis-à-vis their southern neighbour. Canada is the world's second largest country in territorial expanse and has a vestigial border with the fourth largest, the United States. The Free Trade Agreement with the United States, popularly approved by Mulroney's victory in the November 1988 election, will make the border even more porous and indistinct. Climate and the magnetism of the American economy have led to Canada's 25 million people being strung out along the border in the most attenuated linear growth known to any country. Ontario has more in common with Michigan than it has with Quebec and, in the west, British Columbia, Washington State and Oregon form a cultural grouping of their own.

Defeating the Quebec secessionists was a political triumph

but the accommodations which had to be made by 'British' Canada placed the Crown somewhat at odds with the search for Canadian nationality. The strains were manifest in the late 1960s when the 'one Canada' platform of Trudeau and the Liberals was pitted against the adherence of the Conservative leader, Robert Stanfield, to the 'two nations' concept of Canada, with a special status for Quebec. In 1969 Prince Philip decided that a few home truths had to be told. The monarchy existed in Canada not for its own sake but for the benefit of the Canadians. If Canadians decided the system was unacceptable, then it was up to them to change it. 'I think the important thing about it is that if at any stage people feel that it has no further part to play, then for goodness sake let's end the thing on amicable terms without having a row about it.'[1]

Much the same could be said in Australia. When the Labour Party returned to power, Bob Hawke backed away somewhat from his remark made in the margins of the 1981 Melbourne Commonwealth summit that the Australian monarchy would be 'phased out' by the end of the century. By the second half of the 1980s he was not so sure. Becoming a republic was not going to make all that much difference to the ordinary Australian. There might, too, have been a feeling at government level that it was not a good time to alienate the 'Brits' by emphasizing a desire to cut the link with the Crown. As Britain moves deeper into the European Community from 1992 onwards it will become increasingly valuable as an interlocutor. Many Australians will tell you, however, that it is only a matter of time before the Crown's constitutional role is ended, in New Zealand as well as in Australia. George Winterton, Associate Professor of Law at the University of New South Wales, begins his 1986 book *Monarchy to Republic*[2] with a blunt declaration: 'This work commences from the premise that an Australian republic is inevitable. Not imminent, admittedly, but inevitable nonetheless.' He argues that because the Head of State is a symbol of national identity, many Australians feel that their retention of the monarch of their country's former 'colonial overlord' in that role detracts from their sense of national identity.

Sir Zelman Cowen, the Provost of Oriel College, Oxford,

who was Governor-General of Australia from 1977 to 1982, advances a different reason for what he sees as a cooling of the relationship. 'The thing that runs for the republic is that the Queen is an absentee head of state, and in a modern state people ask "How does it make sense?" '[3] He sees no way round that problem.

The appointment in August 1988 of Bill Hayden, Hawke's Foreign Minister, as Sir Ninian Stephen's successor as Governor-General could not exactly be described as a plus for the Australian monarchy. Hayden is no lover of the Commonwealth, no Anglophile (he comes from Irish-American stock) and has expressed republican views. One of his first announcements on acceptance was that he would break with precedent and decline a knighthood. However, he withdrew earlier criticism of the Governor-General's task as being largely confined to 'opening fêtes and attending baby shows'. He regretted his remark, he said; it had been made in the heat of the moment at the time of the 1976 sacking of Gough Whitlam's Labour Government by Sir John Kerr, the then Governor-General, following a deadlock between Senate and government over the budget. 'I would have no problems being governor-general on behalf of the people of Australia for the Queen of Australia.'

As in Canada, the remaining constitutional links with the British Parliament and the Judicial Committee of the Privy Council have been ended in Australia. Also as in Canada, the old Anglo supremacy is being eroded by immigrants from elsewhere than the British Isles. Equally it is true of both countries that the great majority of people are not much bothered by having a British monarch as head of state. It may be increasingly anomalous, but it costs very little and everyone knows Australia is a completely independent country; the *Spycatcher* case has provided abundant proof of that to even the most grudging republicans. The fervent supporters of monarchy may not be great in number, but then neither are the fervent opponents. Polls indicate that in recent years republicanism reached a peak of about 40 per cent of the electorate in 1976, at the time of the Kerr-Whitlam dispute.[4] It dipped to around 30 per cent, but in 1989 appeared to be once again on the rise.

One of the curious things about the Queen is that no Commonwealth leader is on record as ever having said a harsh word about her. Her image is utterly benign and dedicated. She and Mrs Thatcher may have had differences, but they do not emerge in even the scantiest form on the 'I said to her and she said to me' level. The Crown, as represented by the Queen, is not robust in its public manifestation (robustness is left to Prince Philip, the Prince of Wales and the Princess Royal, who speak their minds on issues they have cultivated) but its existence at the centre of things in the Commonwealth is constantly affirmed to all, for the most part on television, by frequent progresses through small and insignificant as well as large and important member states. As the functional side of the Commonwealth has diminished, shedding trade and defence ties, the Crown has become increasingly important as a point of reference in a system where much is nebulous. What A. Berriedale Keith wrote in the 1930s of the relationship between monarchy and Empire remains essentially true today:[5]

the most important and vital link of Empire is the person of the king and the crown. Moreover, the existence of the king solves effectively the relationship between the parts of the Commonwealth. Were it not for the Crown it would become necessary to seek to formulate definitely the relations between the several parts.

The New Zealand Prime Minister, David Lange, updated that conclusion in a 1986 interview:[6]

The Queen is the bit of glue that somehow manages to hold the whole thing together. She has a quiet but fairly pervasive presence at social functions. She is intelligent and acute when she speaks with Commonwealth leaders, to my judgement, and yet when it comes to a functional role, it is not there. She is very careful not to exercise that functional role which would be destructive of the bond, and I suppose it is to some extent a matter of worry that clearly her personality is a major factor to all of us in the Commonwealth. She does the unifying.

Future (and present) problems

What worries Lange, presumably, is that the unifying factor is not the institution of the Crown *per se* (as it still was in the 1930s) but the fact that the leaders of the Commonwealth are fond of and have considerable respect for the wearer of the Crown. The principle has been personalized. So what happens when the Queen goes? Is all that affection automatically transferred to Prince Charles, or do the Old Commonwealth countries decide that the reign of Queen Elizabeth was a transitional phase between the end of the Empire and their emergence as fully fledged countries and that they no longer need a foreign monarch as their Head of State? The Queen is, after all, essentially the Queen of the United Kingdom. She and her family between them own some eighteen residences in England and Scotland, but none of them keeps residences abroad (or even in Wales and Northern Ireland, for that matter). If Her Majesty's Commonwealth subjects want to see the Crown jewels, the Fabergé collection or the royal stamp collection, they have to go to London. There is nothing of permanence outside Britain.

Fiji in 1987 showed how tricky the relationship can be. The Queen's Prime Minister, Dr Bavadra, had been overthrown in the interests of Melanesian supremacy in a country where half the population is of Indian origin. The Melanesians of Fiji were (and perhaps still are) among the Crown's most devoted loyalists. The Indians have no noticeable affection for either the Crown or Britain. But the only way in which the Queen could have honoured the loyalty of the Melanesians and kept the Crown of Fiji would have been by endorsing the unconstitutional entrenchment of Melanesian supremacy. The Queen as Head of a Commonwealth in which the bulk of the population is Indian could hardly have acted in that way even if she had felt an overpowering desire to do so. If Fiji had already been a republic, it would still be in the Commonwealth. Equally, if it had merely suspended the constitution, as happened in Grenada when Maurice Bishop's leftist dicatorship took over following the 1979 revolution, it would still be a monarchy and still in the Commonwealth. But because the curious rules of the Commonwealth stipulate that a country which ceases to be a monarchy must reapply for membership under its new status as a republic, Fiji was out, refused readmission, and the Queen had lost a crown.

South Africa left the Commonwealth on a similar point, changing from monarchy to republic and then withdrawing its application for readmission. What would have happened if the Nationalists had decided for tactical reasons to remain a monarchy? Would the Queen, in the face of Commonwealth hostility to apartheid, have felt obliged to abdicate the Crown of South Africa in order to force the issue and preserve the Commonwealth? Under Commonwealth rules, the internal affairs of a member State cannot be discussed, but it is hard to imagine the African members exercising the sort of hands-off discretion they showed over the internal affairs of Afro-Caribbean Grenada.

It is worth recalling that the Crown did not lose South Africa for lack of trying to keep it. As with the Church of Rome, it is the survival of the institution which matters primarily, not the context in which it survives (since that, it is argued, may change for the better if the institution survives). The Crown may have its social democratic manifestations on occasions, but it is essentially a conservative institution whose roots tend to go downwards rather than sideways in their search for nourishment. John Wheeler-Bennett, the biographer of King George VI, has called the King's visit to South Africa in 1947, his last to one of his dominions before his death in 1952, a 'great imperial mission'.[7] It was essentially a mission to save Smuts and the Crown of South Africa. There was in reality already little hope for Smuts, and even if he and his brand of politics had survived defeat by Malan and the isolationists of the National Party in 1948 it would have been merely a respite. More notable than the trip in a way was the broadcast dedication of her life to the Commonwealth made by the heiress to the throne (both princesses went on the tour) from Cape Town to mark her 21st birthday.

I declare before you that my whole life, whether it be long or short, shall be devoted to your service and the service of our great Imperial Commonwealth to which we all belong. But I shall not have strength to carry out this resolution unless you join in it with me, as I now invite you to do; I know that your support will be unfailingly given.

The Queen's enthusiasm has remained constant. In the month following the Vancouver summit, when the stresses tearing at the Commonwealth's fabric were evidently still much in her mind, she used a speech at the Commonwealth Institute's Silver Jubilee celebration to distance herself from criticism in Britain and reaffirm her own position. The summit had attracted, as usual, much attention in the media, not all of it positive, she noted. 'By contrast, I have no reservations about being the Head of a group of nations which stand, as I said on a much earlier occasion, for "the highest qualities of the spirit of man".'

Her visits overseas since she came to the throne have been weighted in favour of Commonwealth countries by a ratio of two to one. Her commitment even expressed itself on one occasion in quasi-political terms, through her Christmas 1983 broadcast (when the televised version included a conversation with the late Mrs Indira Gandhi on development issues), in a concern about the North-South divide: 'One of the main aims of the Commonwealth is to make an effective contribution towards redressing the economic balance between nations.' The Christmas broadcasts have been a substantial element in the monarchy's relationship with the Commonwealth ever since the first one was made by King George V in 1932. Only very rarely do they fail to include some direct reference to the Commonwealth or some body associated with it. In the Queen's case the only exception since 1980 was in 1986, when the message concentrated on the theme of Christmas as a festival for children. Whether her son's commitment is equally tenacious is questionable. He has not publicly dedicated himself to the Commonwealth's welfare, nor has there been any specific attempt in his speeches to build himself up as the future Head of the Commonwealth. As someone who knows him put it:

It is not a matter of policy. He's a different creature from the Queen, that's all. His interests are the inner cities, the environment, architecture. He's very fond of Australia – his year at Geelong [the famous boys' school near Melbourne] was a marvellous experience for him. But the Commonwealth is not at the top of the list of what turns him on. And after all, it's the Queen who is Head of the Commonwealth, not he.

Even if there is no policy of putting a little space between the heir-apparent and the Commonwealth, it makes sense to avoid over-identification with an institution whose future is uncertain. Prince Charles goes on tours of Commonwealth countries, in particular keeping alive the Australian connection with no less than seven visits since the Kerr-Whitlam crisis, but touring is, after all, part of the family business. There has, though, been a clash of interests with the Secretariat caused by his wish to live in Marlborough House, the home of his great-great-grandfather, Edward VII, when he was Prince of Wales. Kensington Palace, where Charles now lives, is not so central and does not offer as much privacy for his family as Marlborough House and its garden. It would have been ideal from his point of view if the Secretariat's eviction during the current rebuilding could have been made permanent. The matter produced a rare rebuff by the Queen to her son. She said, 'No'. The Secretariat was entitled to Marlborough House and she wanted it to stay there if that was the general desire. 'She told him he would have to put up with Kensington Palace until his turn came to move into the big house [Buckingham Palace]', said an observer.

The Queen's opposition to the move may have been stiffened by a feeling that ousting the Secretariat would have been interpreted as a downgrading of the importance of the Commonwealth at a time when Mrs Thatcher's rough handling of it at the 'sanctions summits' had already lowered its status in British eyes. Despite her views, the matter seems not to have been finally resolved in the Secretariat's favour until the meeting of senior Commonwealth officials in the Seychelles in late 1988. The Foreign Office dropped pressure on the Secretariat to move out of Marlborough House as part of a reorganization only after Ramphal had pointed out that its right to occupy Marlborough House was written into the Agreed Memorandum. 'Pacta sunt servanda', (treaties must be observed), he is said to have intoned.

Charles's apparent avoidance of too close an association with the Commonwealth may be a matter of inclination rather than policy, but it marks him out as belonging to a different era of royalty. Not only his mother but his grandfather and great-grandfather, too, were embodiments of the Commonwealth ethos, with the Raj central to the preoccupations of George V and George VI. Both were Emperors of India, George V the only one to be proclaimed at his own durbar in Delhi, George VI the last of the line. It was a crown which the usually distinctly unmilitant George VI was reluctant to surrender. He was angered by the proposal of Lord Wavell, a wartime viceroy, to release Nehru and Gandhi from gaol and 'amazed' when Churchill told him that all parties in Parliament were prepared to give up India after the war ended. 'I disagree and have always said India has got to be governed, and this will have to be our policy.'[8] For Charles, Europe may turn out to be a more important arena than the Commonwealth, as was the case with Edward VII. His visit to France in November 1988 was generally regarded as a triumph which recreated a geniality and warmth lost or chilled in the Euro-battles of the past decade.

Historical training

If one seeks to trace the evolution of the House of Hanover/ Windsor into an international monarchy 1860 is a good year from which to start. Canada had been vested in the Crown following the Indian Mutiny; the steamship had made even the most distant parts of the Empire relatively accessible (people were already talking about distance having been 'annihilated'); and the Prince of Wales, the future Edward VII, was 18, old enough to be entrusted with a diplomatic mission of the ribbon-cutting, tree-planting kind. Thanks to his high-minded father, Prince Albert, and his educational adviser, Baron Stockmar – the Kurt Hahn (of Gordonstoun) of his day – Edward was being taught kingship on lines suited to a constitutional monarch apolitically dedicated to the progress of his peoples. The opportunity to provide him with practical experience of what lay ahead came when a deputation from the Canadian government (which had provided an infantry regiment for the Crimean War) visited Queen Victoria and invited her to tour Canada and lay the foundation stone of the new parliament building in Ottawa. She replied that it was a long, time-consuming journey and there were too many risks to make it feasible, but she would in due course send her eldest son.

It was an idea which had already been promoted by the Duke of Newcastle, Palmerston's Colonial Secretary, who was alone in the Cabinet in believing imperial ties should be strengthened.[9] Some churlish souls in the Colonial Office, in fact, complained that it would be better if the ties were slackened. As soon as the Canadian trip was known about in Washington, President Buchanan (who had spent three years in London as the Minister of the United States) invited the Prince to spend a few days with him in the White House before returning home. The invitation was accepted, as was one to New York, and on 9 July 1860 the Prince sailed for Canada from Southampton aboard *HMS Hero* accompanied by the Duke of Newcastle, the Earl of St Germans, Lord Steward of the Royal Household, Gen. Robert Bruce, the Prince's governor, two equerries, a physician and two journalists, the correspondent of *The Times*, Nicholas Woods, and an artist, G. H. Andrews, of the *Illustrated London News*. It was the first visit of its kind. The new, travelling royal family, complete with attendant press, had been born.

At more or less the same time it was arranged that the next in line, Prince Alfred, should lay the foundation stone of the breakwater in Cape Town harbour. 'What a charming picture is here', Prince Albert wrote to Baron Stockmar, 'of the progress and expansion of the British race and of the useful co-operation of the royal family in the civilisation which England has developed and advanced.'

The visit was a great public relations success. The *Times* correspondent wrote column after solumn which appeared after much delay, sometimes prefaced by complaints about the state of communications. The first royal shock-horror story appeared in the American press: an account of how the Prince had had to be rescued from the incoming tide while fishing. At Niagara Falls he was reported to have been sportingly inclined to accept an offer by Blondin, the high-wire artist, to be wheeled across in a wheelbarrow. That insatiable desire to see, touch, dance with, dine with and read about royalty was also being born. The Prince was indefatigable on the dance floor. In New York tickets for the ball in his honour were sold by scalpers for $150 and so many turned up that the floor threatened to collapse. A Canadian minister, Sir John Rose, thought the visit taught Canadians that royalty was no longer 'the stern and unapproachable thing they were accustomed to consider it'. That personal, oddly intimate relationship with royalty was to persist even in the remotest corners of Empire despite the republicanism which developed in Britain in the vacuum created by Victoria's seclusion following the death of Prince Albert in 1861. Charles Dilke, who had republican leanings himself, recorded with surprise his arrival at Pitcairn Island in the Pacific in 1866: 'As the first man came on deck, he rushed to the captain, and shaking hands violently, cried, in pure English, entirely free from accent, "How do you do, captain? How's Victoria?"'[10]

Parallel with the 'human face of royalty' aspect of the Prince's visit to Canada was something opportunist and probably not planned with any great deliberation, but nevertheless of considerable diplomatic significance: the visit to Washington. Buchanan saw to it that Edward, the great-grandson of George III, planted a chestnut tree near the Mount Vernon grave of George Washington, the man who deprived King George of an empire. 'The simple but solemn ceremonies at this consecrated spot will become an historical event and cannot fail to exert a happy influence on the kindred peoples of the two countries', the President wrote to Queen Victoria. A new relationship to succeed the tensions and animosities created by two wars had been symbolically established, and it was to survive the severe strains imposed on it by incidents such as the Trent case (when two commissioners of the Confederate States were taken off a British vessel by a Union warship) during the Civil War which broke out in April 1861.

But how modern was the modern monarchy really? One can stand in the Durbar Room at Osborne House on the Solent and wonder at the desire for pomp and tribute whch prompted

Victoria to have it built. The bone-white brilliance of the moulded plaster of the ceiling and walls holds the light from that short-lived fantasy which gave four British monarchs the right to assume an exotic but entirely alien title to an empire. 'Victoria, Regina et Imperatrix', the Queen signed herself delightedly in her letter of thanks to Disraeli after the passage of the 1876 Bill which put her on the same exalted footing as her imperial relations in Central Europe and Russia. The Durbar Room is a late manifestation of Victoria's romance with India, built in the decade after her 1887 Jubilee. Around its walls are the portraits of rajahs and ranees, thakores and maharajas and artisans and risaldars and servants, including the devious 'Munshi', Abdul Karim, who tried unsuccessfully to teach her Hindi in her old age. Hindi was one of *her* imperial languages and it appears on an equal footing with Gaelic, Latin and English in the quadrilingual inscription on Albert's equestrian statue on the edge of Smith's Lawn in Windsor Park.

Like other monarchs before her, the Queen assumed a rather unrealistic protective relationship with her conquered subjects. The Holy Roman Emperor Charles V ordered his conquests in the Americas to cease until a special commission decided if they were just, and Victoria was almost equally solicitous. 'The Indian people should know there is no hatred for a brown skin, none', she wrote to the Governor-General, Lord Canning, when power was transferred from the East India Company to the Crown after the Mutiny, '... the greatest wish on this Queen's part [is] to see them happy, contented and flourishing.' She disapproved of the original wording of the proclamation of her sovereignty on the grounds that 'it seemed to assert England's power with needless brusqueness'. Such a document, she wrote to the Prime Minister, Lord Derby, 'should breathe feelings of generosity, benevolence and religious tolerance, and point out the privilege which the Indians will receive in being placed on an equality with the subjects of the British Crown, and the prosperity following in the train of civilisation'.[11]

It may have been the motherly Crown, but it was thoroughly imperial. Victoria disapproved of the idea of competitive examinations for posts in the Indian Civil Service because it affected her right to make appointments which had delegated powers from the Crown; and she believed the army should be under her control, through the commander-in-chief, rather than subject to the orders of the new Indian Council. Disraeli had told her in a letter about the 1859 India Bill that the bill was 'only the ante-chamber of an imperial palace' and she would do well to take the steps which would impress her name upon her subjects' 'native life'.[12] She was to take up that idea in the 1870s and Disraeli poured his oriental tinsel on the faery queen by pushing through Parliament in the face of fierce opposition the bill which made her Empress of India. She came down to dinner on the evening of the day of the proclamation, New Year's Day 1878, glowing and coruscating with the gems and jewellery showered on her by Indian princes, and Disraeli, violating etiquette, toasted her as Empress of India 'in a short speech as crowded with imagery as a Persian poem, and the Queen, far from being scandalised, responded with a smiling bow that was almost a curtsey'.[13]

Monarchy and Empire had been united to the great benefit of the former's prestige and popularity. This was the peak of the monarch's glory and fame and it is possible to see in the modern Commonwealth, and the emphasis placed on it in the reign of Queen Elizabeth II, an attempt at compensation for the loss in 1947 of the Indian Empire, such a prestigious and extraordinary adjunct of the Hanoverian-Windsorian Crown. As the world's only international monarch, the Queen has a glamour and uniqueness which renders the Crown virtually impregnable at home. Without the Commonwealth, the monarchy would sink into the humdrum homeliness of its Scandinavian brethren and its cost to the taxpayer would be increasingly questioned. 'Value for money' thinking might well be applied to the Crown with the unflattering rigour suffered by other institutions. But until the Commonwealth either fades away or changes into a different sort of association – one which does not require the linkages of sentiment and symbolism provided by the British Crown – world leaders will continue to be flattered by royal visits and humbler ones will still look upon them as a seal of approval. The millions spent by British governments on the Civil List, the royal yacht *Britannia* and the Queen's Flight pay for international public relations as well as the United Kingdom's Head of State and her family. The monarchy, in short, is still 'value for money' in British terms. The Commonwealth, other than Britain, pays nothing for its Head; nor do the Commonwealth monarchies in which the Queen is Head of State, except of course the salaries of their governors-general and the cost of the monarch's visits to her realms.

Queen Elizabeth's accession to the throne more or less coincided with the short-lived belief of post-war British governments that the Commonwealth would help redress the imbalance between Britain and the superpowers. The Queen, even before she was enthroned, affirmed her loyalty to it. The Commonwealth remains a realm in which the Crown has more jurisdiction over its travels and more confidence in the validity of its opinions, than it has elsewhere in the world, where it is held on a tight leash by the Prime Minister and the Foreign Office. But the Queen is planning to cut down her travels as she grows older and the Commonwealth will see less and less of her. With the Prince of Wales and his siblings to share the burden, the Palace and the Foreign Office will have no shortage of royal 'assets' to show off. But as the monarchy and the Commonwealth change, so very probably will the adhesiveness of the 'glue' to which David Lange referred. Measuring the inclinations or tendencies of the post-Elizabethan monarchy by categorizing the countries visited by the Crown Prince may be questionable science, but it is still interesting. Although in the years between 1966 and 1979 the proportion of Commonwealth to non-Commonwealth countries visited by Prince Charles was roughly three to two, in the years since 1980 the proportion has been almost reversed.

9
The Institutions: Crumbling Edifices, Changing Uses

IT IS curious that in a city so abundantly provided with monuments and memorials there is nothing in London which marks the passing of the old Empire. No commission has sat to consider a monument; no sculptor or architect has been inspired. Official imagination seems to have stopped at the grey marble plaque unveiled by the Queen in Westminster Abbey cloisters in 1966 which commemorates 'all those who served the Crown in the colonial territories'. But if you look for something slightly different, a monument to mark the transition from Empire to Commonwealth, there is one ready-made in Collcutt's tower, all that remains of the Imperial Institute, once the heart of Albertopolis, the magnificent complex of science, music and empire between the Prince Consort's memorial in Hyde Park and the Natural History Museum. John Betjeman had to fight hard to preserve it when the rest of T. E. Collcutt's building was torn down to make way for the new Imperial College, a place with all the elegance of a municipal bus station. The tower stands free on a plinth of low steps, 300 feet of creamy stone interrupted here and there by rings of red brick, a slight acknowledgement of the Indian sources of much of the money that built it in its projecting balconies and occasional arches. Queen Victoria laid the foundation stone, Paarl granite on a pedestal of Indian bricks, on 4 July, 1887, before an audience which included the kings of Denmark and Greece, the crown prince and princesses of Germany and Portugal, the Infante and Infanta of Spain, at least eleven Indian princes, and innumerable members of the royal families of Britain and continental Europe. The Prince of Wales, President of the Institute, presided at the ceremony and Sir Arthur Sullivan wrote and conducted the music for an ode written by the Welsh poet Lewis Morris (Lord Tennyson, the Poet Laureate, declined, pleading indisposition) and sung by the Royal Albert Hall Choral Society. It contained a verse which might (with due allowance for its reference to kinsmen etc) reasonably be considered the first, and probably only, Commonwealth anthem.

No more we seek our Realm's increase
By war's red rapine, but by white-winged Peace;
Today we seek to bind in one,
Till all our Britain's work be done —
Through wider knowledge closer grown,
As each fair sister by the rest is known,
And mutual Commerce, mighty to efface
The envious bars of Time and Place,
Deep-pulsing from a common heart
And through a common speech expressed —
From North to South, from East to West,
Our great World Empire's every part;
A universal Britain, strong
To raise up Right, and beat down Wrong —
Let this thing be! Who shall our Realm divide?
Ever we stand together, Kinsmen, side by side!

The Institute's first director, Sir Frederick Abel, inventor of cordite and author of *The Modern History of Gunpower*, saw it as helping in the struggle to beat off increasing competition from Britain's commercial rivals. It was to be a 'great central source of information' for all, investors, merchants, artisans and intending emigrants, with conference rooms, libraries, map rooms, reading rooms and a commercial intelligence department modelled on the military one of the War Office. More than £400,000 was raised to build it, nearly a quarter of it from India; and the roof leaked from the outset.

You can climb up Collcutt's tower — more properly known as the Queen's Tower — by alternating iron and stone spiral staircases, through the empty and unused (apart from a rather limited exhibition of the old Institute) chambers, past the great peal of bells inscribed with the name of their donor, a Mrs Elizabeth Millar of Melbourne. Then, at last, you look out from the topmost balcony over London. From there you can just see in the distance, to the west, the patched copper roof of the Institute's successor, the Commonwealth Institute, in Kensington High Street. Its roof leaks, too, or did until it was repaired. Its round, pavilion-style design and tent-like roof convey an impression of transitoriness, as if it could quite suddenly be taken down and removed, and the impression is not entirely unfounded. It is here that the unfinished saga of 'Commonwealth Place' is unfolding.

A major review of the Institute's work was carried out in 1986 at the behest of the Foreign Secretary. A number of radical changes were made, a plan was drawn up, a 'major funding programme' launched in the following year with the support of industrial and commercial backers – and then, suddenly, the Institute found itself trapped in a government-created dilemma. The Institute is not a government organization, but it depends on money provided through the Foreign Office for rather more than 60 per cent of its total receipts, a percentage which has declined rapidly since 1983–4 when it was 83 per cent. Its budget is modest: about £3m. a year. After 18 months of negotiation between the Institute and the Foreign Office, when everything was ready to breathe life into a revitalized organization fit to face the 1990s, the Foreign Office abruptly cut its grant-in-aid in an imposed settlement. The Institute was the victim of public expenditure cuts. Raise the difference yourself, was the message from the Foreign Office. In the absence of a firm government commitment the sponsors shied away and by the beginning of 1989 the Institute was negotiating with several developers with a view to forming a partnership for a commercial development of Commonwealth Place.

The Institute's aims are to increase knowledge and understanding of the Commonwealth, its nations and peoples, and at the same time to promote educational and cultural co-operation and understanding. Thousands of schoolchildren troop through the tiered interior each year to see exhibitions from every Commonwealth country and territory. The administrators hope to increase the use of the Institute, draw in more support from sponsors and boost revenues by 3 per cent a year. The beflagged site, set back from Kensington High Street next to Holland Park, has become Commonwealth Place, the Library and Arts Department have been merged in the educational side of the Institute's work, and old-style multiculturalism, with the emphasis on the variety and distinctiveness of the member nations, is out. Instead, the emphasis is on the things, such as law, language and institutions, which unite the Commonwealth.

Despite its title, only 3 per cent of the Institute's funds in 1986–7 came from Commonwealth countries other than Britain, although they spend substantial amounts on their exhibitions. In the 1988–9 financial year grant-in-aid from the Foreign Office was cut by 5 per cent; it will be cut by a further 12 per cent in 1989–90. Add inflation, and the cut amounts to a large slice of core funding. The staff, who numbered 149 in 1979, dropped in 1988 to just over 90. 'All this makes pretty good mockery of some of the things we were told in autumn last year [1987] when it was agreed that to achieve our objectives we needed 125 staff', says Richard Bourne, the Deputy Director.

The Foreign Office has sacked many of the old board of governors and appointed new ones. A recommendation that the Commonwealth High Commissioners should be removed from the board (on which they sit by right as representatives of their countries) was diplomatically abandoned. The senior staff of the Institute would have liked the new chairman to be a businessman, but the FCO insisted on putting in one of their one, a retired diplomat, Dick Fyjis-Walker, former Ambassador to Pakistan, a lapsed Commonwealth member.

It was a psychological rather than a financial blow when the Australian High Commission telephoned in late 1987 to say that their government had sent instructions that it was pulling out of the Institute with immediate effect. 'Do you mean you want the flag pulled down and the Australian exhibition removed?' asked the amazed Director, James Porter. The answer was 'yes'. The move appears to have been part of an Australian cost-cutting exercise aimed at multilateral organizations. It was also, according to an Australian official, 'because we consider the Institute a British affair'. It took intervention by Sir William Heseltine, the Queen's Private Secretary, who is an Australian, and others to get the instruction partly rescinded by Bill Hayden, the then Australian Foreign Minister. The flag did not come down. The Australian Bicentennial Exhibition went ahead at the Institute, but the High Commissioner did not turn up to open it.

'The Australians are quite entitled to ask for value for money', says Mrs Lynda Chalker, the Foreign Office Minister responsible for Commonwealth affairs.[1] And, indeed, the British Government's attitude is very little different. 'Value for money' is a phrase which crops up frequently in any discussion with her of the Commonwealth's institutions. There is a firm belief among the staffs of some of them that the Old Commonwealth governments, led by the Australians and the British, are secretly in league to trim organizations to the size and shape dictated by reduced needs and altered objectives. In Chalker's opinion the Commonwealth Institute has largely itself to blame for its predicament; it should have made the necessary decisions about its future earlier and not waited. But points of that sort made about a largely government-funded organization are obviously arguable, particularly when the government encourages and approves change and then fails to keep its side of the bargain. When Sir Patrick Wright, the Permanent Under-Secretary at the Foreign Office, was questioned at a Foreign Affairs Committee hearing on the FCO's attitude to the Institute, his less than enthusiastic tone made it reasonably clear that support for it was not on the government's list of priorities. 'We continue to support the Institute but we have to make an allocation against the total amount of money available.'[2]

Other institutions

However one views the story of Commonwealth Place, it reveals a government whose attitude, when choices have to be made, is uncompromisingly hard-headed towards a troubled bastion of the Commonwealth ethos. Nor is it much worried about giving offence, even to the Queen, whose presence ensured a good turnout by the affluent and influential for the launch of the funding programme at the Institute's silver jubilee reception on 9 November 1987. But toughness apart, there is a question of the viability and usefulness of a number of Commonwealth organizations. Periodically, the Secretariat publishes what is described on the cover as 'a directory of official and unofficial organizations active in the Commonwealth'. The latest one came out in 1985. It has 266 entries divided into two parts, official and unofficial organizations, and in many cases (the Carnegie Corporation of New York and The Friends World Committee for Consultation, for instance) the Commonwealth link seems extremely tenuous.

The enquirer who attempts to use the directory to investigate how much is real and how much illusion or vanished may find himself in for a frustrating time, with an unusually high number of dead lines, phones that ring without answer, answering-machines and changed numbers. The first entry in Part 1 (official organizations) is the Commonwealth Advisory Aeronautical Research Council, whose address is given as c/o Ministry of Defence, Whitehall. Neither it nor the Commonwealth Defence Science Organization (also listed as having an office in the Ministry of Defence) could be traced through the ministry's switchboard, information desk or press office, or through British Telecom's directory enquiries. They apear to have vanished without trace. The Commonwealth Air Transport Council was contacted without too much difficulty in the Transport Ministry, but is nevertheless in limbo for the time being. Its activities overlap with ICAO (the International Civil Aviation Organization) and at the September 1987 meeting of the Council in Ottawa a special committee was set up to consider whether the organization had outlived its usefulness in its present form and to make recommendations on its future role. By contrast, the Commonwealth Telecommunications Organization seems to have adapted and survived quite well. Equally, the Commonwealth Press Union flourishes, although it can hardly be called a notable champion of press freedom. Membership is corporate, not individual; complaints are taken up only when the request comes from the aggrieved party; and the only publicity protests receive is through the *CPU Quarterly*.

Three pages of Part 1 of the directory are occupied by the 'Commonwealth Agricultural Bureaux' and their four institutes, of mycology, entomology, parasitology and biological control. The latter is listed as being sited in Trinidad, but in fact it left in 1984 – 'It was a bit out of the way for an international organization', explains the Director, Dr Greathead – and is now to be found in Imperial College's recently opened Silwood Park campus near Ascot.

What has happened to the bureaux, founded in 1928 to provide information and scientific services in agriculture, is an instructive story of adaptation and survival, fitting for an organization involved in pest control and genetics. They have moved their headquarters from Farnham Royal to new premises at Wallingford (where the 11 bureaux can be centralized) and changed their name to CAB International, retaining the 'Commonwealth' of the old name only in an unexplained capital 'C'. The change – which includes a new constitution permitting broader membership – was made to enable the organization to register as an international organization with the United Nations, which it did in January 1988, thus entitling CABI to talk to the big UN agencies, such as the World Bank and the UN Development Programme. It has thus widened its horizons and its opportunities and in late 1988 was negotiating membership with 12 non-Commonwealth countries, among them Hungary, West Germany and Japan. Commonwealth membership had proved too restrictive and ever since the oil price rise of 1974 it had been hard to get members to raise their contributions. The inevitable problems caused by moving premises, in 1987, were exacerbated by a £1m. budget deficit. Despite that, contributions were held down by the member states, principally Britain, to only 4 per cent increases (based on a low estimate of UK inflation); savings were made by cutbacks and curtailment of longer-term projects, accompanied by a drive to hold on to existing markets and to improve what the organization has to offer. CABI has a staff of over 400, half of them scientists, and an annual budget of £10m., 80 per cent of which comes from the sale outside the Commonwealth of its highly respected abstract journals (member states get them free) as well as research work and consultancy services. The remaining 20 per cent comes from Commonwealth countries, nearly a quarter of it from Britain.

There used to be two Institutes of Commonwealth Studies (both are listed in the directory), one in Oxford, formerly the Institute of Colonial Studies, the other a part of the University of London. London survives, Oxford has gone. The Oxford Institute was housed in Queen Elizabeth House, founded under Royal Charter in 1954 to serve as a research and residential centre for the study of developing countries, including the Commonwealth. After a new building was completed in 1961, the Institute and Queen Elizabeth House more or less merged, the latter's warden serving as the Institute's director. The government funded Queen Elizabeth House through the Overseas Development Administration until 1985–6, when it persuaded the university to take it over. The Institute foundered because it was seen as no longer serving a useful purpose and Queen Elizabeth House now has no specifically Commonwealth function. Instead, it houses the International Development Centre, an amalgam of several organizations.

By contrast, another Oxford institution with Commonwealth, or perhaps imperial, links is doing rather well, Rhodes House, founded on South African money in the interests of realizing Rhodes' dreams of creating a master-race of Teutonic imperialists to run the world, is, surprisingly, listed in the directory. It has faced some internal difficulties because two of the South African schools with which the Trust is associated are all-white and segregated. But that does not seem to have deterred any of the 200 scholars sponsored by the Trust. Nowadays they come from India, Pakistan, Nigeria, Kenya, Hong Kong, Malaysia and Singapore as well as West Germany, South Africa (nine students, including one black and one Asian), the United States and the Old Commonwealth.

The London Institute of Commonwealth Studies has survived what its 1986–7 annual report calls 'alarums'. The great Australian financial pull-out threatened to close its

Australian Studies Centre, established only in 1982. The Centre's Australian Head, Professor Tom Millar, blamed Bill Hayden, the then Foreign Minister, and his gut anti-Britishness. Despite an impressive array of academic support and yet another intervention from Sir William Heseltine, Hawke did not override Hayden; instead, he claimed that he had persuaded the Menzies Foundation to pick up the bill from July 1988. The Centre's Chairman Sir Zelman Cowen, a fellow Australian of equal distinction, disputes Hawkes' claim. 'I was astounded when I heard they were planning to cut off funding from the middle of the bicentennial year and I wrote and told Hawke it was a great mistake. I fought against it and I got the money from the Menzies Trust.'[3] The university is committed to safeguarding the Institute's academic activities 'so far as finances allow'. It enjoys a lonely eminence as the only institute of its kind in the world and has been granted the equivalent of probate over the Empire's last testament, the establishment of a nationally supported project for publishing British documents on the end of Empire, known semi-acronymically as BDEEP.

The Institute of Commonwealth Studies represents the young Commonwealth, with graduate students from here, there and everywhere (and not just the Commonwealth) passing through its fan-lighted Georgian doorway in Russell Square, Bloomsbury. Less than a mile away, in Northumberland Avenue, the heads which pass through the portals of what was until the beginning of 1989 the Royal Commonwealth Society are distinctly on the venerable side. Renamed Commonwealth House, this is the social hub of the Commonwealth, the occasional haunt of former colonial governors and pertinacious ladies whose questions at meetings indicate liberal opinions unchanged since the intellectual fashions prevailing on the eve of decolonization in the 1940s and 1950s. It is the place where visiting Commonwealth prime ministers go to speak and it has an excellent specialist library built up since the loss of most of its original collection by enemy action in the Second World War. The atmosphere is club-like, faded, but pleasantly homely to those who know it, with a restaurant, bar, bedroom accommodation for 80 members, and a situation (next to Whitehall and Trafalgar

Square) which would put a price of many tens of millions on the building if it were ever sold.

Founded in 1868 as the Colonial Society, the eventual RCS became the Royal Empire Society before anchoring itself in the Commonwealth rather late in the day, in 1958. It survived being struck in 1941 by a 4,000 lb bomb which gutted the building (by Lutyens' partner at Delhi, Sir Herbert Baker), destroying the library and the precious panelling and woodwork contributed from all round the Empire. That was made good so far as it could be, with Sir Herbert called in again and with more gifts of exotic woods. At the end of 1987 it faced a more insidious threat: a sizeable overdraft and a trading loss in the year of £187,000. A combination of an ageing membership, under-use and a widening gap between income and expenditure had brought the RCS to that wrenchingly familiar Commonwealth condition where assets, function and the future had to be urgently reviewed in the context of a changed world.

The RCS's co-habitant at Commonwealth House, the Victoria League for Commonwealth Friendship, founded in 1901, faced a different sort of problem: plenty of money but not enough to spend it on. The membership of 2,800 sounds healthy, but many were elderly and some had been paying the same low subscription rate for the past 50 years. Its function had been to arrange hospitality with British families for Commonwealth visitors and families. That task was handed over, with a payment of £10,000 a year, to a government organization, HOST (Hospitality for Overseas Students), which has an office in Commonwealth House and caters for students from anywhere in the world whether Commonwealth or not.

It became obvious that the sensible thing would be to merge the RCS and the League. The Victoria League bought a £500,000 slice of the equity of Commonwealth House from the freeholder, the RCS, and the two organizations were merged in the autumn of 1988 as the Commonwealth Trust, although still retaining their separate charitable identities. 'Both organizations were getting a bit tired', said Michael McWilliam, a former chief executive of the Standard Chartered Bank, who stepped in as the RCS's temporary administrator in 1987–8. 'The royals recognized there was a need for change.'

The royals are no small factor in the affairs of Commonwealth House, providing an unsinkable life raft of patronage as it searches for dry land. The Queen and the Queen Mother (who, with her husband, then Duke of York, opened the building in 1936) are patrons of both the Victoria League and the RCS. The Duchess of York is Grand President of the RCS and Princess Margaret has the same position in the Victoria League. At the beginning of 1989 a trio of knights took up position below this formidable array. Sir Zelman Cowen, fast moving into the position of leading champion of Commonwealth causes, became President of the Trust; Sir Peter Marshall, a former diplomat who retired at the end of 1988 as Deputy Secretary-General (Economic) of the Secretariat, took over the chairmanship; and Maj. Gen. Sir David Thorne was appointed Director-General.

'Whitehall is behind us', said McWilliam. 'It sees us as a useful place for meetings, press conferences, as a sort of second string to Lancaster House.' The Pall Mall clubs were doing rather well, and there was no reason why Commonwealth House should not draw on new members, but refurbishing it to attract younger people to make good use of it was going to cost 'several millions'. There were signs of movement in other directions in early 1989. The West India Committee, a venerable body whose main concerns are trade and investment, became the first Commonwealth-related organization to take office space in Commonwealth House and the Foreign Offie backed the Trust's efforts to set up a Commonwealth Liaison Unit with a modest one-off grant of £7,500.

One of the Trust's goals is to make itself 'Britain's leading NGO' (non-governmental organization), a term heard frequently these days in Commonwealth circles. It is an ugly acronym for an undescriptive label. Much thought has been given to finding a better way of describing voluntary private organizations engaged in humanitarian and similar types of work, so far without success. International organizations like the World Bank and several Western governments (including Britain, whose contributions to NGOs came to £42m. in 1988) rely increasingly on them rather than inflating their own bureaucracies, but this carries the recognized danger that ambitious but inadequately staffed NGOs will overreach themselves. And in Third World countries some NGOs, far from being non-governmental, are in fact government-controlled. Despite problems of this sort, many see them as the way ahead for a Commonwealth whose essence is a network of personal relationships and voluntary organizations which will prove more trustworthy and durable than the quasi-political structure created by the Secretariat and the heads-of-government meetings.

The RCS has been active in pressing the case for the 'non-governmental Commonwealth'. An essential element required to knit it together is the Commonwealth Liaison Unit (CLU), a somewhat evasive concept in which the Commonwealth Foundation (for promoting co-operation between professional bodies and other NGOs) has been involved. In fact, the establishment of a network of CLUs is the principal task confronting the Foundation, according to its Deputy Director, Joseph Tsang. CLUs are intended to promote co-operation between NGOs and governments and among NGOs wherever they may happen to be in the Commonwealth. Despite the Foundation's interest in the subject over several years, no CLU was actually established by the beginning of 1989, although the one at the Commonwealth Trust and another in the Solomon Islands were moving ahead satisfactorily. There were, in addition, 15 others spread around the world that had been 'identified', according to the Foundation. 'It is not an easy thing to set up', said Tsang. 'Sometimes there is an excess of enthusiasm when two NGOs want to take over the same CLU and we have to wait until they sort things out.' Shortage of equipment, including typewriters and computers, had been another obstacle, but Tsang remained confident that all would be sorted out before long.

The Commonwealth Parliamentary Association

One indication of the attitude of British politicians towards the Commonwealth is that there is no Commonwealth lobby, no equivalent of the old Empire hands of the Tory right who used to be so vociferous about Kenya and Rhodesia and who can still be heard defending South Africa, no Tory 'wet' version of Julian Amery. Tony Durant, Conservative MP for Reading West, sounded slightly surprised at the suggestion that it indicated a lack of enthusiasm:

There's no need for a lobby because there's no opposition to the Commonwealth. People speak up for various bits of it, Australia, India and so on, but no one speaks for the Commonwealth as such. There is considerable latent support for it, though, and I see it growing in strength. It's shifting away from the old white Commonwealth towards the smaller countries, who, after all, are the majority.

Durant, a Tory whip, is chairman of the UK Branch of the Commonwealth Parliamentary Association. It makes a change to listen to an outspoken optimist about the Commonwealth and the CPA is one of the few Commonwealth institutions which appears to be trouble-free. Politicians like meeting one another to talk and exchange ideas; and they like travel, too, of course; Kuala Lumpur for the annual conference in 1987 and Canberra in 1988. 'The CPA is very trips-oriented', said a British MP. The association has a working capital fund which pays for the travel of politicians from the poorer countries. Moreover, membership is open to any country, province or state which has a parliament. The four Channel Islands and the Isle of Man are members, as are the component assemblies of India and the Australian and Canadian federation. At the 1988 Canberra conference the total of assemblies represented came to a remarkably high 115 from 45 countries and their dependencies. Some of these are the smallest and poorest countries in the world and since the beginning of the 1980s they have taken to holding their own conference in advance of the main one. Since size is the criterion, the mix is an unusual one, with wealthy Prince Edward Island, one of the Canadian Maritime Provinces, and the Cayman Islands, the bankers' haven, sitting down with impoverished Kiribati and Nauru.

Dr David Tonkin, the CPA's Secretary-General, is a former

Liberal premier of South Australia. He claims an apolitical position when it comes to one-party states and whether some of the members measure up to the association's objective of respect for the 'positive ideals of democracy'.[4] In his view, the African one-party states are 'adaptations' of the Westminster model. In any case, there is a better chance that the democratic processes will work if everyone can get together and talk. At the end of 1988 four of the Commonwealth's 15 African members were 'in abeyance', as the CPA delicately phrases it when a military or some other form of dictatorship takes over and dissolves parliament: Uganda, Nigeria, Ghana and Lesotho. In a different category of 'abeyance', but nevertheless with their parliaments suspended, were three Indian states and a union territory: Punjab, Nagaland, Tamil Nadu and Mizoram (territory).

The CPA has its headquarters in a grace-and-favour office in Old Palace Yard, Westminster, provided and furnished by the British Parliament. It has a membership of 8,500 of the Commonwealth's 12,000 parliamentarians and through its seminars and regional conferences provides a forum where parliamentary sheep and goats can mix to what is, hopefully, the latter's advantage. Democracy is an uncertain vane in many parts of the Commonwealth but even the one-party states have democratic aspects which are cherished by enough people to make them worth encouraging.

10
The Sporting Commonwealth

'IS DON Bradman still alive?' enquired Nelson Mandela when Malcolm Fraser saw him in Pollsmore Prison.[1] Even by 1964, when Mandela was sentenced to life imprisonment, Bradman had long ceased hitting either headlines or boundaries, but he nevertheless remained a symbol of Australian prowess in Mandela's mind, the sort of person one could comfortably bring into the initial chit-chat with a visiting Australian ex-Prime Minister. Sport is what most of the Commonwealth has in common as much as the English language, more so than the law or institutions; and Mandela's South Africa, it should be remembered, was still in the Commonwealth until only a few years before the gaol doors closed on him and played its last Test series against the Australians, in South Africa, in 1970. The games they play add up to one reason why the Australians are closer to Britain than the Canadians, who play neither cricket nor rugby, and that in turn helps explain why the Canadians are the umpires of the Commonwealth. The South Africans play both games with fervour – particularly rugby, the national game of the Afrikaner – and ostracization has hit them as hard as the arms embargo. Sport and politics are never far apart in the Commonwealth.

The career of John Emburey, briefly the England captain, provides a good example of what the South African connection can mean to a cricketer.[2] Emburey was in the England XI during the 1980 West Indies tour when a replacement, Robin Jackman, who had played and coached in South Africa the year before, had his entry permit revoked on arrival in Georgetown, Guyana. The 1977 Gleneagles agreement (of which more later) on sporting contacts with South Africa was invoked. The second Test in Georgetown was cancelled and the remainder of the series played in other West Indian countries, which, after a few days for thought, decided Gleneagles did not apply. There was similar trouble in advance of the 1981–2 India tour, when Delhi announced that Boycott and Cook were unacceptable as members of the England XI because they were on the UN blacklist for having played in South Africa. They were able to take part in the tour only after they had accepted Mrs Indira Gandhi's proposal that they make a public rejection of apartheid. It is thus astonishing that Emburey and others, including Graham Gooch, should have signed up in 1982 for a secretly arranged (largely by Boycott) tour of South Africa by an unofficial England team. But they did, and were duly stunned by the fury of the reaction. For a player like Emburey, at the peak of his career, the three-year ban from England selection imposed by the Test and County Cricket Board on the rebels was an exceptionally severe punishment. He lost three profitable overseas tours and some 15 home Test matches at £1,500 a time. The money earned in South Africa did not compensate, even though it was enough to 'take the heart out of a fairly substantial mortgage'.

Banning may have been a deterrent to some, but in April 1988 the UN blacklist contained no less than 136 English male players, 24 women players and an entire Oxford and Cambridge University team of 15 including their manager. The blacklist (properly called *The Register of Sports Contacts with South Africa*) is an impressive document comprising several thousand names collected from a wide range of nations by anti-apartheid activists and either sent direct to the UN Centre Against Apartheid or the London-based South African Non-Racial Olympic Committee (SAN-ROC). Sam Ramsamy, SAN-ROC's Executive Chairman, estimates that almost 25 per cent of the English county registered players go to South Africa during the British winter. Few have much prospect of playing Test cricket, so the blacklist does not worry them. The South Africans are grateful for any foreign players even if they are mediocre, and they get paid more than in England.

Matters came to a financial head in the late summer of 1988 when the England selectors produced their team for a winter tour of India. Eight of the 16, including the captain, Gooch, and the vice-captain, Emburey, were on the blacklist. Despite the fact that some of the eight had visited India to play in the 1987 World Cup, the Indian government made it reasonably clear from the start that none of them would be granted visas. In fact, the Sports Minister, Margaret Alva, declared that she would sooner have the tour cancelled by the TCCB than allow Gooch to play in India, and she was supported in this by two former Indian captains, the Nawab of Pataudi and Bishen Singh Bedi.

There was a certain consistency in the TCCB's refusal to allow India to select who could play and who could not: England had abandoned a tour of South Africa exactly 20 years earlier when it refused to accept a veto of South African-born Basil D'Oliveira on the grounds of his colour. But the decision in January 1989 of the International Cricket Conference to end once and for all participation in international cricket by players who coached or played the game in South Africa clinched the matter. The agreement may have saved England from being forced out of international cricket, but it also meant there was no longer much incentive for the South African Cricket Union to continue its attempts to hold the banners at bay by desegregating the game.

There was a hidden factor in the Indian position on the England team which had been speculated on from the start of the row but which remained unconfirmed until 9 September 1988, when the decision not to grant visas to the eight was formally announced by the Foreign Ministry in Delhi. The Commonwealth Games Federation was due to decide on 15 September on who would host the 1994 Commonwealth Games, and Delhi was campaigning hard for the privilege. Unnamed sources in the Sports Ministry admitted that a desire to win African votes for Delhi had been a reason for the rejection of the eight.[3]

The Commonwealth Games

The Games are not only one of the most engaging features of the Commonwealth, they are arguably its second most important gathering, ranking after the summits and ahead of other ministerial meetings. This is the great wapenshaw of the Commonwealth, when the athletic regiments are paraded in a mood of cheerful celebration which, say those who know the Games well, is found nowhere else. If the rest of the Commonwealth foundered or simply faded away, they would probably still continue. It is a testimony to their underlying strength that they have survived their entanglement with politics in the 1970s and 1980s and have not been permanently damaged by the fiasco of the Edinburgh Games of 1986, when African and other Third World countries carried out a boycott in protest against Mrs Thatcher's refusal to impose comprehensive sanctions on South Africa. 'There's a mystique about them', explained one enthusiast. 'There's so much camaraderie, and, of course, everyone can communicate, because they all speak English.'

The Games are staged every four years half way between the Olympic Games. Once they came second only in size and importance to the Olympics, but in recent years they have been overtaken by the Asian and Pan-American games. This slippage has not diminished the competition among Commonwealth cities to hold them; Perth, Australia, and Cardiff had already, in 1988, put themselves in the running for the 1998 Games.

There was a sports meeting during the 1911 Festival of Empire, but the present-day Games were really born during the 1928 Olympics at Amsterdam. 'The Olympic Games were really getting terribly tough', said Sandy Duncan, the Librarian of the Commonwealth Games Council for England, and unofficial historian of the Games. He has attended every one of them apart from the first in Hamilton, Ontario, in 1930, and competed in 1934 and 1938. Bobby Robinson, the Canadian team manager, approached Empire colleagues at Amsterdam with Hamilton's offer to stage Empire games and there was agreement that they would be 'much nicer, not nearly as tough, and we would enjoy them'. The founders met in London and announced that the Games would be modelled on the Olympics in structure and would keep to the same strict definition of what constituted an amateur.

But the Games will be very different, free from both the excessive stimulus and the babel of the international stadium. They should be merrier and less stern, and will substitute the stimulus of novel adventure for the pressure of international rivalry.

Six sports were selected for Hamilton: athletics, bowls, boxing, rowing, swimming and diving, and wrestling. There are now 14 sports on the list, but only ten are permitted at any one Games, with athletics and swimming compulsory. From the start, Britain sent separate teams from its component nationalities as well as from Jersey, Guernsey and the Isle of Man. At the 1982 Brisbane Games there were competitors from 46 countries or dependencies (out of 63 members of the Federation) and even the Falklands managed to send a representative. As Duncan explained:

One of the nice things is that the bigger countries help the weaker brethren. At Edmonton (1978) the man the Bangladeshis sent to do the horizontal bar couldn't do the grand circle, so the English coach taught him. Then there were the Cyprus girl gymnasts who had never been on the beam. The Canadians took them on. Everyone competes as an individual and there is no national medal count, but I can tell you that England has had the most medals.

It was this homely encounter, the 'Friendly Games', as they are billed, that Rajiv Gandhi wanted to win for Delhi. However, according to some, he left it too late. By the time everyone got to the Seoul Olympics, Victoria, British Columbia, which had fought off competition from eight other Canadian cities anxious to hold the 1994 Games, had put together a financial package and presentation which left Cardiff and India in the shade. Victoria, the Province of British Columbia, the Canadian Government and Canadian business had between them offered subsidies and backing worth tens of millions of pounds, it was claimed afterwards. There were charter flights to pick up the competitors from

African and other poor countries, money to kit them out and help with their accommodation, and offers of free training. The voting on these occasions is secret and no one is obliged to say who they voted for. The discretion at Seoul was more than usually opaque. Victoria won hands down in the first round, by 29 votes to India's 18 and Cardiff's 7. The Third World, including, it was suspected, a number of African countries, had obviously defected en masse to the First World in the shape of Canada.

The Indians erupted in fury. They claimed that the Canadians had spent $8.5m. on lobbying alone and had bought a swarm of Caribbean, Pacific and other poor States with their promises. Mrs Alva refused to commit India to competing even in the 1990 Auckland Games. Earlier, during the presentation of the Indian bid, she had declared, 'A vote against India would amount to a vote of no confidence in the developing countries, a suggestion that we are not capable of playing a role as an equal partner'. The Indians had a case. The Games have only once been held in a Third World country – in Kingston, Jamaica, in 1966. All the rest have been in the four Old Commonwealth countries, with three of them in Canada. The Games were in the grip of a 'colonial concept', Alva complained.

It was 'quite remarkable' for Delhi to lose out, admitted David Dixon, the British Hon. Secretary of the Federation, reflecting on events afterwards in London. 'It would be much healthier for the future of the Games if they were to go outside the white Commonwealth.' What had really counted in the end, he thought, was the proven ability of the Canadians to run the Games. Duncan took a different view of why matters went as they did. 'There were the problems of innoculations and vaccinations and all that sort of thing if they were held in India. It will be a lot of fun in Victoria.'

Others described the situation more explicitly in terms of gastric problems. Even if left politely unvoiced at Seoul, the thought of India's invincible bacteria and their ability to home in on alien stomachs was clearly for many people a more important reason for not going to Delhi than poor presentation or doubts about Indian organizing ability.

According to Duncan, the Games were free of politics up to

and including the 1966 Kingston Games. After that, Southern African began to intrude. Rugby, not cricket, became the issue, specifically the New Zealand All Blacks and the South African Springboks. The Montreal Olympics of 1976 was the first battleground, with Julius Nyerere, supported by the Supreme Council for Sport in Africa, theatening a boycott unless New Zealand withdrew. The New Zealand Prime Minister, Robert Muldoon, was a conservative libertarian who was prepared to discourage contacts with South Africa but not to ban them. More to the point, perhaps, he had scant respect for the Nyereres of this world. The New Zealand team was not withdrawn from the Olympics and eventually 32 African and other Third World countries boycotted them. This was the background to the 1977 Commonwealth summit in London and the Gleneagles Declaration.

The Gleneagles Declaration

Sporting relations with South Africa were actually a secondary issue at the summit compared with Rhodesia and what Idi Amin (who did not attend despite blustering threats to do so) was doing in Uganda. Nevertheless, Gleneagles is what the summit is remembered for in Commonwealth circles and the declaration has become a seminal document, frequently cited and variously interpreted. It saved the Edmonton Commonwealth Games in the following year, which was the immediate intention, much to the relief of the Canadians who did not want another Montreal on their hands. Only the Nigerians, who were chairing the UN Committee on Apartheid at the time, boycotted them, but boycotts and allied measures were by then becoming an integral part of what the Nigerians assumed to be their natural leadership of black Africa. Even as recently as May 1987 they pre-empted any suggestion of a decline in their militancy by announcing that they would boycott the 1990 Auckland Games if South Africans were included in the British team.

Gleneagles was the venue for the summit's weekend retreat, where a drafting committee which included Trudeau, Muldoon and Brig. Joe Garba, the Nigerian Commissioner for

External Affairs, was deputed to draw up a declaration which could be agreed by consensus. What emerged has to be seen in relation to the earlier Singapore Declaration of Commonwealth Principles (born out of the row at the 1971 summit over Heath's plan to renew arms sales to South Africa, a rather more serious issue than games between the Springboks and the All Blacks. This affirmed the rights denied by apartheid and recognized racial discrimination as 'an unmitigated evil of society'. All were pledged to afford no assistance which directly contributed to the pursuit or consolidation of apartheid. Sporting fixtures with South African teams were seen in that light. The Gleneagles Declaration 'drew a curtain across the past' with an agreement that governments would withhold support for sporting contacts with South Africa and take 'every practical step' to discourage them. Implementation of this commitment was left to individual governments to decide within the terms of their own laws.

The Commonwealth Games Federation elaborated the agreement into a code of conduct when it met at Brisbane during the 1982 Games. This laid down what constituted a breach of the Gleneagles Declaration (everything from planning to participation in any sporting event with South Africa), made suspension by the Federation from participation of any sort in the Games the punishment for a breach, and appointed the national associations as the watchdogs of the Declaration. The code ended with a ringing statement that in view of what had been agreed, including the Federation's power to punish, 'the Games should not in future be jeopardised'.

The Brisbane code was a by-product of the previous year's Melbourne summit, where New Zealand rugby had been a central issue following Muldoon's refusal to withhold visas for the visiting Springbok team. The Commonwealth finance ministers moved their meeting from Auckland to the Bahamas as a result and as a curtain-raiser to the summit Ramphal accused Muldoon in an article in *The Times* of being 'somewhat less than vigorous' in discouraging the Springboks and of calling in the military to ensure the tour went ahead in the face of violent protests. Muldoon's reaction was forceful: the article was 'an unfortunate combination of hypocritical platitudes and downright misstatements'. Gleneagles' purpose was to discourage sporting contacts, not to prohibit them. The New Zealander's loathing of both Ramphal and Fraser, the host at Melbourne, came through loud and clear during the summit. He up-staged their Melbourne Declaration on North-South economic co-operation with a press conference of his own denouncing it as a 'series of pious platitudes' with a 'totally inadequate conclusion'. The Declaration, issued in the name of the summit and intended to lend strength to the North-South summit in Cancun, Mexico, which immediately succeeded it, was indeed a string of homilies, but such documents are usually passed over quickly with a suitably reverential comment or two; it was rare to hear a prime minister rubbish one with such enthusiasm. Even Robert Mugabe, attending his first summit as Prime Minister of Zimbabwe, came in for a lashing over an adverse comment on the Springboks' tour. 'I suppose when you have been in the jungle for years shooting people you can't understand. He's got a closed mind.'

The Edinburgh fiasco

The Edinburgh Games in 1986 were to prove the most traumatic of the thirteen held since 1930. The Australian government had picked up the £17m. bill for the Brisbane Games. The Edinburgh Games, in line with the British government's unsentimental sink-or-swim-but-don't-expect-a-lifebelt-from-us policy, were the first to be commercially sponsored. The only subsidy had come from the Edinburgh City Council, which refurbished the Meadowbank Stadium at a cost of £4m., but, following a change from Tory to left-wing control, the pledge of a further £4m. was not honoured. A fund-raising consortium had started with hopes of gathering in £12m. of the basic £14m. running costs through commercial sponsorship. The Los Angeles Olympics, it was pointed out, had paid their way through sponsorship, TV rights and sales. But Commonwealth Games do not get networked in the United States and the sale of their TV rights does not bring in a bonanza; the BBC was the only bidder and got the rights for three years for £450,000. Local commerce showed itself largely indifferent and the consortium fell short of its target by a margin of several million pounds. It is extremely difficult, in fact, to run the Commonwealth Games without backing from government and other public sources, and at Edinburgh the British government refused to underwrite any losses.

The Games were soon being described in the press as 'troubled' and Robert Maxwell, the publisher, was hurriedly made their co-chairman once it was clear there would be no government help. He claimed that only his acceptance stopped the receivers from being called in within days. If that had happened, said Maxwell, 'Scotland would have had a nervous breakdown and the UK would have been humiliated beyond belief'.

In fact, the UK was being humiliated, but not beyond belief given the history of sporting politics. The Africans and their allies were organizing a graduated boycott, in protest against Mrs Thatcher's policy on sanctions and the inclusion in the English team of Zola Budd, the runner, and Annette Cowley, the swimmer, both South Africans with British passports. Nigeria and Ghana pulled out first followed by Uganda and then Kenya and Tanzania. India joined the boycott with the start of the Games only four days away. The Games opened on 24 July with only 26 countries participating, the lowest figure since 1954 and 20 less than each of the two previous Games. Among the Africans, only three took part: Botswana, which never adopted the Front Line States' position; Lesotho, which first joined the boycott and then changed its mind; and Malawi, whose leader, Dr Banda, opposes sanctions and would willingly have allowed Budd and Cowley to represent his country, if that had been possible. Maxwell revealed a month after the Games that the debt came to £4m. and the row with the creditors has dragged on until early 1989.

The Africans and the anti-apartheid movements have thrown a sports blockade around South Africa, which they patrol vigilantly. One can regard it as an infringement of the rights of individuals to choose where and with whom they want to compete or coach. Or one can see it as a bloodless means of exerting pressure on an unjust society which hates ostracization. Unlike economic sanctions, it is overwhelmingly whites who suffer. Some black sportsmen feel they are doubly victimized, discriminated against at home and barred from competing abroad (since the ban is total and not based on colour), but they are relatively few. The question is not whether the blockade is technically effective, which on the whole it is, but whether it is politically effective. The most remarkable evidence that it is having an impact came in October 1988 when the high priests of Afrikaner rugby, the veteran Dr Danie Craven, President of the South African Rugby Board (SARB) and Louis Luyt, the fertilizer magnate who heads the Transvaal Rugby Union, met Thabo Mbeki and other senior African National Congress officials in Harare.

What had driven the Afrikaners to make such a journey was the increasing restlessness of players and their supporters at being locked into their own corner of the world, away from the rapturous excitements of matches with the Lions and the All Blacks. The last Springbok tour abroad was to New Zealand in 1981. Attempts to put together a rugby alliance with the unlikely name of the Gondwanaland Rugby Federation[4] with Chile, Argentina, several other Latin American countries and possibly some of South Africa's black satellites do little to slake the thirst of the rugby playing public for red-blooded competition with traditional rivals. Craven and Luyt came back from Harare with an agreement that all-white SARB and the non-racial South African Rugby Union (SARU) should merge to form a 'genuinely non-racial national rugby federation'. SARB and SARU were brought together at the meeting, but SARU, although said to be sympathetic to Craven and Luyt, is affiliated to the South African Council on Sport (SACOS), which is not. 'No normal sport in an abnormal society', is SACOS's war cry. During the last months of 1988 President Botha was conducting his own forays north of the Limpopo in an attempt to explain his country's affairs and demonstrate that he could meet African leaders. But in his canon, and that of most of his white countrymen, talks with the ANC amount to dealing with terrorists and are unacceptable. Nor is it likely that the government will proceed further down the road of liberalizing sport to introduce the complete desegregation which SACOS and its supporters demand. SARB was soon brought to heel and gave an abject promise there would be no more meetings with the ANC. Nevertheless, the Harare meeting was significant in that it happened at the initiative of white South African rugby officials, and it undoubtedly gave the ANC a considerable propaganda boost.

Ramsamy, an Asian born in Natal, considers that tremendous progress has been made. He has no quarrels with the imposition of political boycotts like the one on the Edinburgh Games. 'Sport is not a sacred cow and never will be.' His estimate is that the financial cost to the South African government of its sports-related propaganda, subsidized tours, tax concessions covering 90 per cent of the cost of sponsored visits, and support for South African sporting bodies (including, he says, SARB) comes to $100m. a year, and is increasing.

Sport matters to the white electorate mentally and physically. It's the only way they have an international dimension. The ban on contacts told them for the first time that they are not wanted. It was the first boycott that began to bite and it has caused the biggest dent in the wall of apartheid – a bigger dent than banking or arms sanctions.

11
The Mega-Problems of Mini-States

PRESIDENT MAUMOON Abdul Gayoom of the Maldives had planned to go to Delhi in early November 1988 to discuss closer ties between his country and India. In the event, Delhi came to him, so to speak, in the shape of 1,000 paratroopers and three warships sent to save his government from overthrow by a sea-borne coup. The leader of the coup, Abdulla Luthufi, did in fact manage to instal himself in the President's office for a few hours before the Indians' arrival forced him and less than 50 Tamil mercenaries to flee in a commandeered freighter in the direction of Sri Lanka, whence they had come. They were soon captured and brought back to the Maldivian capital Malé to await trial. It was the third coup Gayoom had survived, and the second in which Luthufi, a poultry breeder living near Colombo, had failed.

India was one of four countries Gayoom turned to in his hour of need. His own National Security Force, lightly armed with pistols, had proved no match for the invaders. President Jayewardene of Sri Lanka responded by saying that he had his own Tamil problems and had no troops to spare. The British (the Maldives were a protectorate until 1965) and the Americans were unable to help. The Indians, on the other hand, who see themselves as the regional superpower, were eager to step in rather than have some troublesome adventurer set up an unstable tyranny on their doorstep.

The invasion was the sort of mini-state crisis that the Commonwealth Secretariat had been preparing itself for ever since the 1983 Grenada affair in the Caribbean had caught everyone off their guard. When Ramphal promptly telephoned Jayewardene and Rajiv Gandhi, telling the latter that Indian intervention would have Commonwealth support, he was acting in line with the recommendation of the Commonwealth Consultative Group's report in 1985 on the vulnerability and other problems of small states:[1]

In the event of a particular security crisis arising for a small member state, we would urge that the Secretary-General should immediately initiate consultations with that government and with the member states in the region in order to ascertain whether there is a general wish for some kind of pan-Commonwealth action and to enable him to formulate appropriate proposals.

The action was not exactly pan-Commonwealth; the Indians would have acted regardless of whether Ramphal had telephoned with Commonwealth approval. But the fact remains that Gayoom was kept in the presidential chair by a fellow Commonwealth country and there were no arguments and recriminations of the sort that five years earlier had followed action by a global superpower, the United States, to restore order in its Caribbean backyard by ending a bloody armed takeover of Grenada, which is both a Commonwealth country and a monarchy with the Queen as its Head of State. India is non-aligned and has impeccable Third World as well as Commonwealth credentials. Diversion by the Americans of a small task force from the vicinity of the Gulf to deal with Luthufi and his Tamils would inevitably, regardless of the worthiness of the objective, have led to protests about imperialist intervention.

If the Commonwealth has any important issue other than the ending of apartheid close to its collective heart, it is the security of small states. Of the world's 44 states with populations of around one million or less, 29 are in the Commonwealth. They constitute the bulk of the organization's membership, and some 16 or 17 of them are so diminutive or poor or vulnerable, or even all three, that it is questionable whether independence is much more than a courtesy title conferred on them by Britain in its haste to leave on the outgoing colonial tide. In reality, they are not much different from the protectorates established by the Great Powers, most notably Britain, in the nineteenth century to save them from worse fates or merely to ensure that a rival did not get its hands on them.

The lessons of Grenada

Grenada at least demonstrated in 1983 that the Commonwealth had underestimated a problem that was in many ways uniquely its own. The Americans had stepped in without advance notice to the British (who had granted the island independence some nine years earlier), but with the physical support of other Eastern Caribbean Commonwealth islands. The Commonwealth's Delhi summit, which came only a month after the US intervention, was notable for a split on the issue between the Afro-Caribbeans and the Africans, led by Mugabe, who insisted that it was a violation of international law, a blatant act of imperialism intended to halt the march of socialism in the region. How, he asked, could Commonwealth Caribbean countries participate in such an undemocratic action? Kaunda came to his support, insisting that a failure to condemn the Americans would lay African states open to the same fate as Grenada. They would be 'thrown to the lions'. The plea by Eugenia Charles, the Dominica Prime Minister – 'do not ignore us, we had no alternative' – was ignored.

Thatcher also thought the intervention bad in principle, even though Maurice Bishop had been murdered, the Cubans had entrenched themselves in the island, were building a large airport which might or might not have had strategic uses, and had supplied arms. She availed herself of an interview on the BBC World Service to declare, 'If you are going to pronounce a new law that wherever communism reigns against the will of the people ... the United States shall enter, then we are going to have really terrible wars in the world.'

This was Thatcher at her worst, allowing nationalism piqued by US intervention in a British preserve to distort her judgment. It was not the Commonwealth's finest hour, either.

Intervention by the Americans and their East Caribbean allies may have produced mixed blessings (a former leader, Sir Eric Gairy, has become a power in the land once again and the cost of the marathon trial of those accused of murder threatens Grenada with the prospect of becoming the first country to be bankrupted by its own legal processes) but, far from suppressing democracy, it at least gave Grenada the chance of returning to it. The inaction favoured by Britain and most of the other members of the Commonwealth would have led to a worsening of the situation.

Grenada had experienced a steady decline into violent repression and political eccentricity ever since Gairy and his Grenada United Labour Party (GULP) came to power in 1968. His right-wing regime was overthrown in 1979 by Comrade Maurice Bishop and the left-wing revolutionary zealots of the New Jewel Movement, whose inspiration came from the Black Power movement in the United States. The party split and Bishop, three of his ministers and several of his supporters were murdered by an even more extreme military faction. One curious aspect of the incident is that throughout the pro-Soviet revolutionary period, including the short-lived coup, Grenada remained a monarchy, with a Governor-General, Sir Paul Scoon, in place.

'It's a very good question – why?' said Oswald Gibbs, Grenada's High Commissioner in London, laughing at the thought of the marxist-leninist monarchy. Only in the Caribbean could that sort of thing happen. Gibbs had been close to the centre of things in the island for many years as a civil servant and diplomat, with an interlude during the revolutionary years.

I asked Paul Scoon that myself once. He knew Bishop well – played tennis with him two or three times a week, that sort of thing. After Bishop suspended the constitution, he offered his resignation, but Bishop said, 'No, I want you to stay on'. And, in fact, one of the decrees issued by Bishop said there would be a Governor-General.

After Bishop was murdered the new leaders imposed a 24-hour curfew and placed armoured cars at both ends of Sir Paul's drive, but still they did not declare the country a republic. The Americans were able to rescue Scoon and he became the constitutional rallying point, his governor-generalship the only stable institution on the island.

In the few years of the revolution, Bishop took care to keep his Commonwealth connections alive, turning up at the 1981 Melbourne summit, dressed in the dark glasses and austere, tieless garb suited to a revolutionary, and his reasoning about retaining the monarchy was clear. Under Commonwealth rules, declaring a republic would have meant reapplying for membership, opening up the prospect of a veto by Britain and the Old Commonwealth countries. He saw the Commonwealth and the monarchy as certificates of at least semi-respectability, good enough with luck to protect him and his regime against outside intervention – a view which even his murderous colleagues seem to have shared. And that tells us something significant and general about small states, whatever their political complexion: their need for big brothers, and their fear of them.

It would be easy to say that the Indian intervention in the Maldives showed that the lessons of Grenada had been learned and a new era opened in which mini-states had their stability underwritten, but it would not be true. Neither Australia nor New Zealand showed any inclination to intervene in Fiji when Colonel Rabuka's 1987 coup effectively stripped the Indian half of the population of their political rights. The cost of military action would have been too high in lives and political fall-out throughout Melanesia and among the Maoris of New Zealand. Or take another group of islands subject to recurrent attempted coups, the Seychelles, 1,200 miles south-west of the Maldives. Less than a year after independence in 1976 the President, James Mancham, was overthrown by his Prime Minister, France Albert René, in a coup backed by Tanzania, which provided the arms and troops to prevent a counter-coup. President René introduced a left-wing one-party state which has turned out to be a fairly pragmatic survivor amid the turbulent cross-currents generated by East and West, South Africa and its East African neighbours. He is undoubtedly a more convincing and dedicated leader than was Mancham with his frequent absences and his global network of girlfriends. But the fact remains that Mancham was democratically elected in multi-party elections and ruled under a constitution devised by the British to accommodate his rival René, the opposition leader, as prime minister.

Surprisingly, the Commonwealth Consultative Group on the problems of small states makes a commendatory reference to Tanzania's role after rather fatuously suggesting that a Commonwealth peacekeeping force of the sort used in the transition of power in Zimbabwe in 1980 might have been deployed in Grenada during the post-invasion elections.[2]

We also note that in moments of urgent crisis the fraternal links of the Commonwealth have facilitated the provision of direct military aid. For example, Tanzania gave support to Seychelles in 1977 ... and we feel this is a worthwhile practice that should continue when the occasion demands.

Which, logically, would have condoned Indian intervention in the Maldives if Delhi had decided it was time for Gayoom to go and Luthufi to take his place. And what, one wonders, would be the Commonwealth reaction if Mancham, or someone supported by him, supplanted René with the backing of Kenya? Would a coup to restore the status quo ante be denounced immediately as reprehensible? Judging the moral wrongs and rights of mini-state coups is immensely difficult.

As it happened, the idea of a collective Commonwealth force to keep the peace and supervise elections in Grenada had been written off well before the Consultative Group's report appeared. Ramphal in his report to the 1985 Nassau summit recorded that he had visited Grenada and talked to the other Caribbean governments in January 1984 and 'this possibility was not pursued'. Scoon, who had spent five years in Marlborough House as the Deputy Director of the Commonwealth Foundation before becoming Governor-General on Gairy's recommendation in 1979, had three meetings with Ramphal and told him he was not enthusiastic about the idea. He preferred help from his Caribbean neighbours. The Secretariat provided some administrative assistance to the island at the request of the Governor-General, but it turned down an invitation to send Commonwealth observers to the December 1984 elections on the grounds that they did not meet the criteria for freedom from external interference and pressure set out in the 1983 summit's communiqué.

Although the Organization of Eastern Caribbean States decided post-Grenada to implement the security clause in their 1981 foundation treaty, no force capable of dealing on its own with a determined invasion has been established.[3] There is a joint arrangement involving co-operation between island police forces, but, said Ron Sanders, who was High Commissioner in London for Antigua until 1987 and later went to Oxford to study small island problems, 'Quite frankly, it couldn't swat a mosquito.'

As emotions cooled in the wake of the Grenada affair governments pondered the possibility that a well-armed group of soldiers trained to defeat coups might develop dangerous ambitions and turn its thoughts to mounting its own attempt. That, after all, was the way in which most coups occurred, including that in Grenada. In the view of Richard Gunn, the London High Commissioner for the Eastern Caribbean states, the Grenada affair exaggerated the danger faced by the islands.[4]

At one time the emphasis was on heavily armed squads running around in camouflage suits, but that has been played down. If anything happened we would need the assistance of Britain or the United States. The biggest threat is drugs and against them we look to protection by the coastguard and the local police.

The British and Americans have provided patrol craft and Britain helps with the training of personnel. A British frigate is usually on duty in the Caribbean and there is a modest force of troops and aircraft on hand in Belize. In November 1988 the SAS held a joint exercise with local police in Barbados – the first of its kind – in which they practised the rescue of Britons held hostage by terrorists. According to Gunn:

Britain has never really neglected the Caribbean, but during the 70s it did look as if it was saying, 'Well, they've got independence, so let's get them out of the way.' Perhaps there was a lack of interest and a lack of aid. Now the outlook has changed and Britain has been playing a big part in maintaining traditional links.

The drug problem

More important than Grenada in awakening Britain, the United States and Canada to the vulnerability of the Caribbean islands has been the growing scale of the drug problem. Police and politicians throughout the region have been corrupted, bought up by smugglers and dealers who use the islands as staging posts en route to the United States, Britain and Western Europe. With so much money involved and the islands wide open despite their re-equipped coastguards, it is almost impossible to stop the trade. Some administrations are honest at the top; in others everyone takes a rake-off. 'You can sit on a beach', said Sanders, 'and watch an aircraft fly over and drop its load of drugs into the sea. Then a speedboat comes out, picks it up and dashes off to deliver it, probably to another island.' The tourist trade and the constant coming and going of yachts makes the traffic all the more difficult to stop. It is estimated that 100 tons of cocaine were carried through Bahamian waters in 1987.[5] The official revenues of the islands in the previous year were $381m.; possibly as much as an additional $300m. from drugs passed through the local financial system and another $300m. did not.[6]

The dark underside of this golden swell of money and drugs is the very large number of Bahamian youths who are classified as addicts – as many as 10 per cent, with the figures possibly rising to 40 per cent in the main urban centres of Nassau and Freeport. The name of Sir Lýnden Pindling, the 'black Moses' who has led the country since 1969, may rattle around courtrooms in the United States with a frequency and venom that would destroy any politician elsewhere, but he stays in power because there is built-in damage-limitation in a trade which brings in so much money – and if you are an addict, you may feel you have an interest in keeping things as they are. 'You see a whole wash of new cars, huge houses built by Rastas with marvellous views of the sea', said Sanders, speaking of Caribbean islands generally where drugs have made their impact. 'Drugs money helps keep the economy buoyant. And governments which run islands with buoyant economies aren't voted out. I wouldn't say island economies would collapse without drugs, but you would certainly notice the difference.'

Not all islands are poor or dependent on drugs. The 2,000 inhabitants of the Falkland Islands can expect an annual income of over £50m. by 1997, thanks to licence fees from the colony's fisheries, according to a report commissioned by the islands' development corporation. The Cayman Islands, a British colony halfway between Jamaica and the Yucatan peninsula, can claim to be the largest offshore financial centre in the world, with 17,000 registered companies, more Eurodollar deposits than Switzerland and average salaries of $18,000.[7] At the other end of the scale are the Turks and Caicos Islands, with a population of less than 10,000, where remonstrations by the US Drug Enforcement Agency finally awoke the Foreign Office to the fact that the islands' government from the Chief Minister down had been corrupted by drugs money. The Chief Minister, Norman Saunders, and several of his associates were caught in Miami and sent to prison in 1985. His successor proved little better, and following arson, corrupt land deals, extortion, and an official enquiry, the government was sacked by the Governor in 1986 and replaced by an advisory council. The islands were returned to democratic government after elections in March 1988.

The list of 29 small states drawn up by the Secretariat for study by the 'vulnerability' panel included two larger than the 1 million norm, Jamaica (population 2.3 million) and Papua New Guinea (3.5 million). These were nevertheless regarded as belonging to the mini-state category because of their close relationship with the smaller states in their regions. The largest number, eleven states, were in the Caribbean, followed by the Pacific with eight. Australia plays an active role among the islands of the South Pacific, and the Commonwealth provides a de facto framework for consultation and collective assistance. The regional Commonwealth summit (which should be held at two-yearly intervals) has not been convened recently, and the principal body for political consultation among heads of government is the South Pacific Forum, which is open to a wider array of nations and dependencies than just the Commonwealth and meets annually. The United States and Japan have recently been discussing association with it. The secretariat for the Forum is the Fiji-based South Pacific Bureau for Economic Co-operation. It also acts as the secretariat for the Pacific ACP countries and is the depositary for the South Pacific Nuclear Free Zone Treaty, whose main target is the French test site at Mururoa atoll, but whose provisions are equally unacceptable to the British and Americans.

Co-operation or federation?

One of the problems confronting small states is how to staff and pay for diplomatic missions. Suitable people are often not available and the cost of maintaining a mission in a Western capital or at the UN in New York can be prohibitive. The establishment by the Australians of a joint office close to the UN for four small states – the Maldives, Papua New Guinea, the Solomon Islands and Western Samoa – in 1983 was such a success that Britain and Canada shared the cost of creating a much larger office to take six other states, Belize, Dominica (which had previously been obliged to close its UN mission on grounds of cost), The Gambia, Grenada, St Lucia and the Seychelles. The Commonwealth Secretariat looks after the administration. The users pay 10 per cent of the running costs (at present $700,000 a year) and the rest is met by richer countries. Each country is allowed 450 square feet of space and if they want more they pay for it.

Loose co-operative arrangements may work, but small states are not, despite their vulnerability, easy to weld together politically. The British had been thinking about federating the Caribbean islands since 1876, long before they started in earnest to create an independent West Indian federation after the Second World War. Island leaders, including Norman Manley of Jamaica, were enthusiastic. But the federation fell apart in 1962 after only four years of existence, the *coup de grâce* a 'no' vote in a Jamaican referendum. Eric Williams, the Trinidad Prime Minister at the time, blamed 'centuries-old inter-island jealousies' among other things.[8] The bigger islands had tasted the post-war wealth brought by bauxite, in the case of Jamaica, and oil in Trinidad, and wanted independence without being tied to smaller and poorer islands. There are those like Ron Sanders who bitterly lament the loss of the 1958–62 federation, as in these remarks made at a Commonwealth Institute seminar in late 1988:[9]

If the West Indies Federation had survived ... as a strong, vibrant nation with economic leverage and political clout, would it not, by now, have had at least an acceptable military capability to defend itself from mercenary attack, would it not have been better able to fight for the Presidency of the UN General Assembly [a reference to the defeat of Barbados' Dame Nita Barrow by the Argentine Foreign Minister, Dante Caputo]? And by the same token would it not have been able to make stronger representation for its nationals here in Britain who are subject to institutional as well as individual racism by immigration, by the police, by the press and even by jailkeepers? Would not the goverment of the United Kingdom have to pay greater attention to a strong, vibrant country of six million people than it has to several small territories, most of which have populations of less than 200,000? Indeed, with the opportunities for employment that such a West Indian nation would have provided, would West Indians have come here at all – would they have abandoned the warmth and comfort of the Caribbean for the cold and coldness of Britain?

Only among the six independent members of the Organization of Eastern Caribbean States (OECS) is serious thought being given to federation, limited in this case to themselves. With the exception of Antigua, all have committed themselves to making the necessary sacrifices of sovereignty. They include in their long, curving sweep from north to south the Windward Islands, some of the poorest places in the Caribbean, quite literally banana monarchies, since bananas are their staple export and all, apart from republican Dominica, have the Queen as Head of State. Their deficit in visible trade in 1986 was $1bn. Only aid and loans enable them to survive, and Sanders questions whether they are going to manage that very successfully in an era which includes the arrival of Europe's single market and the US-Canadian Free Trade Agreement. If the OECS countries do not go ahead with political union even the degree of integration which they do possess will, in Sanders' view, begin to unravel and they will find themselves on 'the path of separation and a fate alone'.

The West Indian community in Britain has its success stories, but it is not by and large a happy community. Its middle-aged and elderly members who have managed to save tend to go back to where they were born; their children stay in Britain. And that, says Oswald Gibbs, means divided families. Family ties are, in any case, very often weak and by comparison with Asian immigrants a high proportion of the Afro-Caribbean elderly live alone.[10] Unemployment among blacks is more than twice that of whites, their public image identifies them with drugs and crime, and the incidence of mental illness among the young is high. That is the 'cold and coldness' to which Sanders referred. Yet the dependence upon Britain of groups like the Windward Islands is inescapable and the approach of 1992 has caused violent tremors of apprehension and uncertainty.

Take, for example, the case of Dominica, the biggest banana exporter in the Windwards. Banana cultivation provides a livelihood for 9,000 farmers and their output accounts for nearly 60 per cent of the island's exports.[11] All but 2 per cent of the exported bananas go to Britain, a protected market. But what happens when 1992 throws down the internal barriers within the European Community? There are better places to grow bananas than the Windward Islands, where the soil is often poor and agronomics an under-used science. The bigger 'dollar bananas', the *gros michels* grown in Central America and some of the South American countries, have a 25 per cent price advantage over the Windward Islands' *lacatans*. The latter may be sweeter, delicately flavoured, more suited in size to a child's lunch-box, and generally preferred by the British consumer, but that would not be enough to save them from being overwhelmed by the cheaper dollar bananas, which are imported in large quantities by West German and other European wholesalers who could easily start shifting them to Britain after 1992.

'If the banana industry collapsed the whole economy would collapse', said Richard Gunn, speaking of the Windward Islands. Britain imports more ACP-country bananas, all of them from the Caribbean area, than any other member of the European Community. Geest, one of the biggest British importing firms, estimated the total British requirement in 1988 at 385,000 tons, of which 80 per cent came from the Caribbean; it would have been 100 per cent if Hurricane Gilbert had not caused havoc in Jamaica. Not all Caribbean islands by any means are dependent on bananas. Jamaica's main exports are bauxite and alumina, followed at a considerable distance by sugar, the other ACP staple. Trinidad lives by selling oil and chemicals. But how to protect these small countries in an era when their products are widely available is an immensely complex problem. Four members of the European Community can, for example, claim to be banana producers: France (in overseas departments such as Martinique, in the Windward island chain), Greece (in Crete), Portugal and Spain.

No one yet knows for sure what 1992 will bring, but it is clear that the European Community will continue to provide markets and assistance for the ACP countries. The Community accepted the objectives of the present system, said Dr Dieter Frisch, the EC's Director-General for Development, in London in November 1988, but it had not yet decided how it would implement them. It would attempt to focus thoughts in the new Lomé Convention (which will probably be consolidated into a long-term agreement instead of being renegotiated every five years) on remedying 'structural weaknesses' in production and marketing in the ACP countries. Ideas that 1992 would see the creation of 'Fortress Europe' were 'absolutely absurd'. Even so, the next decade is likely to be a difficult one for the ex-colonial micro-states. Some believe that the poorest, like the Windward Islands, should be allowed a transitional period in which to come to terms with a changing situation in which they will have to diversify into new products and industries. This is an area where the Commonwealth can act, through Britain, as a useful advisory and pressure group. There are no guarantees against future Grenadas, but they are less likely where economies show growth rather than decline.

Hong Kong

Before the repression of the democracy movement in China in mid-1989 Hong Kong would have received no more than a one or two line mention for the simple reason that, although it is a British colony, it lies outside the Commonwealth framework. It is in every respect hard to classify. In size it is a mini-state. In population (5.5 million) it is a small state. But in terms of GNP it is rich – much richer than the great majority of Commonwealth states. In fact, it is a reasonable guess that if one adjusted its GNP to the values of the late nineteenth century, this imperial relic would turn out to be a great deal more valuable than the Raj in its prime. But Hong Kong is a leasehold colony, and when the lease expires in 1997 it will return to China in the form of a Special Administrative Region. What has made it an awkward Commonwealth issue is the claim by 3.2 million of its citizens to right of residence in Britain. The fate of Hong Kong's Chinese and the possibility of a Commonwealth solution was being discussed in advance of the Kuala Lumpur summit. But 1997 is still some years away; the Peking government has still time to mend its brutal ways. It is not politically feasible for Britain to grant right of residence to so many, and it is doubtful whether other Commonwealth countries will want to rush in with offers.

12
The Commonwealth and Britain

IN HUMAN terms the Old Commonwealth is virtually invisible in Britain, its members merging into the background almost without trace. It is a safe bet that few, if any, trouble the Commission for Racial Equality with their problems. They have their chambers of commerce, a sprinkling of clubs like the Maple Leaf, a few pubs that Australians and New Zealanders like to gather in, but generally speaking they go native with ease and do not need to band together for comfort or security. The Australians are the only ones accorded a caricature identity; the hard-drinking, laconic four-X man from the outback who appears in the beer advertisements. The modest Canadians, lacking any suitable natural stereotype, leave their beer advertisements to British actors. The majority of white Britons have friends or relations, near or distant, living in the Old Commonwealth; and, since the Old Commonwealth has no separate institutional existence, its scions who come to Britain to work and study tend to be regarded as a part not so much of the postwar Commonwealth as of the white English-speaking world.

Plazas and predators

Where the Old Commonwealth becomes more visible is in reinforced steel and concrete. The Reichmann brothers of Toronto are building Europe's largest commercial project at Canary wharf in London's Docklands, a chain of plazas and towers of a kind familiar in North America but new to Britain. Some native-born developers regard the scheme as a £3bn white elephant being built at the wrong time in the wrong place. The Reichmanns are unimpressed by the sceptics; they proceed with the confidence of men who have never put a foot seriously wrong in their climb to the top of the world's wealth. Their privately owned company Olympia and York has been variously valued at between £6.5 and £9bn. Its holdings include the £1.2bn World Financial Centre at the Wall Street end of Manhattan (the biggest New York development since the Rockefeller Centre went up in the 1930s) and eight New York office blocks which they snapped up in 1977 when the city's prospects were widely rated as poor and prices were low. The Reichmanns are Orthodox Jews who left Vienna as refugees in the 1930s and came to Canada by way of Paris and Morocco. Despite their wealth, an aura of puritanical modesty pervades their Toronto homes, and they have been described as rich, reticent and religious. The title 'Old Commonwealth' sits oddly on them and almost certainly they would never think of themselves as its representatives. They are, in fact – and this is a general point about the Old Commonwealth and its relations with Britain – no different either in the way they are regarded in Britain or in their attitude towards it from a host of other international businessmen and developers.

On the other side of the West India Docks from Canary Wharf the Reichmann brothers have a Toronto neighbour for whom the Old Commonwealth label does have some value. Conrad Black, owner of *The Daily Telegraph*, *The Sunday Telegraph* and *The Spectator*, houses his newspaper staffs in a sombre example of dark glass post-modernism. Anyone of any nationality can invest in property without question, but the printed, opinion-forming word is a sensitive area of British life which until recently (the stray American has appeared) has been restricted by custom and familiarity to the Old Commonwealth. No continental European has attempted to move in, although there is nothing in principle to stop one doing so. Black had the advantage of being able to fit into a tradition of Commonwealth newspaper proprietors: the first Lord Beaverbrook, proprietor of *The Daily Express*, hailed from New Brunswick and was synonymous with Empire and imperial preferences; Lord Thomson of Fleet, who tried hard with *The Times* and failed, was born in Toronto, from where his heirs run American and Canadian newspaper chains; Rupert Murdoch, owner of the *Sun* and *The Times* stable, may have become an American for commercial convenience, but everything about him is indelibly Australian. Nevertheless, there is no evidence that Black thinks of himself as 'Old Commonwealth'. He owns newspapers in the United States and Canada and his political and personal identification is with North America, not with Britain, much less the Commonwealth.

He backed Mulroney and the Free Trade Agreement in the November 1988 Canadian election and in an article in *The Daily Telegraph* of 19 November dismissed the opposition of John Turner and the Liberals as 'nationalist insularity'. The British connection was 'popular and nostalgic' but not a counterweight to what a former prime minister, Mackenzie King, had once described as the 'overwhelming contiguity' of the United States. The 'French fact' (Quebec) was now as much a threat as a buttress to Canada's political identity. 'Fear of the United States is an unstable and often rather disreputable sentiment in a country that is fundamentally rather pro-American, though anti-annexationist.' Pierre Trudeau and the Liberals spent 14 years promoting the 'Third Option' of increased trade with the European Community and Japan only to see trade with them actually decline by 50 per cent in that period. By contrast, the trading relationship between Canada and the United States was the largest between any two countries in the world. The idea that Canada was more civil, peaceable and 'compassionate' than the United States was dismissed as something that had been fastened on to by 'the elements of the bureaucratic, academic and journalistic communities that, in Canada and elsewhere, exercise an unrepresentatively large influence over the formation of fashionable opinion'. Black, as the reader may guess from the quotation, views liberals with suspicion.

The Free Trade Agreement is North America's answer to the European Community and 1992. There is no such answer for the Australians and New Zealanders, nations created and preserved by a vanished British sea power and, since the middle of the present century, under the aegis of a distant United States. The approach of the 'Year of Europe' may not have given an electrifying jolt to Canadian investors in Britain (although it must have figured in the Reichmanns' calculations), but it has played an important part in stimulating the growth of Australasian investment. 'We don't know yet how '92 is going to turn out', said an Australian High Commission official in London, 'but our gut feeling is that it's better to get a foot in now, and that's how we advise firms.' The most notable heeders of such advice have been the 'Australian predators', a term which until recently would have been applied only to the probably extinct *Thylacinus cynocephalus*, the Tasmanian tiger. The efforts of the brewery chieftains Alan Bond and John Elliott of Elders IXL to take over Lonrho and Scottish and Newcastle respectively provided long-running entertainment on the City pages of the British press throughout 1988. Australian investment in Britain grew by 740 per cent in the five years up to 1988, but it is still only about £3.5bn,[1] small compared with a British investment in Australia which in 1987 came second, only by a small margin, to American investment and stood at about £16bn.[2]

Bicentennial Year 1988 was the year in which Australians formally rejected the 'British cringe' – subservience to the modes and manners of their founder-state on the other side of the globe. Some like Professor Tom Millar, the Australian head of the Australian Studies Centre at London University, found the mood of self-congratulatory nationalism tinged with anti-British feeling 'awful'.[3] For Britons, who have long been told by Australians to regard them as more akin in attitude and most other things to the United States than to Britain, the urge to play down the British connection came as something of a surprise. In fact, Australians are not particularly like Americans; anyone who has lived in old Rhodesia or the Cape will recognize them as belonging to a unique and vigorous sub-culture, British Colonial. This is why, in addition to climate, English-speaking South African whites escaping from the excesses of Afrikanerdom can settle down so happily in Melbourne or any other large Australian city. The human terrain is familiar. Such a comment is not patronizing; it is merely to point out that, although Australia is not 'British', its population still has more in common with the British than with any other people. Seven per cent of the population were born in the United Kingdom ('predator' Alan Bond among them), as Prime Minister Hawke conceded in a speech of welcome to Mrs Thatcher at Canberra in August 1988. The annual migration programme contains twice as many people from Britain as from any other country. But all that has, of course, to be set against the fact that nowadays Australia is down-under not so much to Britain as to the all-conquering economic dynamism of Japan and the expanding population and unstable energies of Indonesia. It is a country which has got its fingertips on the Pacific rim but whose influence is in no way commensurate with its geographical size. Between 15 and 16 million people live in a country the same size as the United States excluding Alaska.

New Zealand, on the other side of the Tasman Sea, has a population of just over 3 million. The ANZUS pact, which long ago replaced the British guarantee, has had a hole torn in it by New Zealand's refusal to allow entry to nuclear weapons, in itself an indication of its willingness to accept isolation from the Western security network. The most important international relationship is with Australia, not with the United States or with Britain, whose entry into the European Community exposed New Zealand to more economic trauma than was suffered by any other Commonwealth country. The Commonwealth has not had much real importance for New Zealand's international relations since the 1970s[4] and Prime Minister David Lange, the 'quiet man' of the Commonwealth summits, has not shown any inclination to change that.

Mrs Thatcher's visit to Australia provided an opportunity to sweep the common ground a little cleaner, pushing the Commonwealth summit left-overs to one side and patting down the resentments aroused by the bicentennial. Hawke's Canberra speech acknowledged that there were significant differences over South Africa but denied that they had prevented co-operation on the great majority of issues dealt with by the Commonwealth. It was very much in both countries' interests that differences were debated openly, understood fully and put in the context of a broader relationship which remains important.

It may seem to some that Australia and the United Kingdom are moving further apart. It is true that Australia is becoming more and more oriented towards the Pacific rim while the United Kingdom has taken the path of closer integration with the European Community. But while these developments offer the prospect of a changed relationship, I am confident it will be a relationship no less important to our future wellbeing. Our long-standing connections with you give Australia an immensely valuable window into Europe. Equally they give Britain a vantage point into the dynamism of the Pacific rim.

Two generalizations can be made about Britain's relationship with the three Old Commonwealth countries. The first is that the Commonwealth is of no institutional importance to it; relations are conducted bilaterally. The second is that no difference which occurs within the wider Commonwealth will be allowed to affect their economic relations; and, therefore, any political damage will soon be repaired.

Within those generalizations there are, of course, differences in the nature of Britain's bilateral relations with the individual countries. A combination of the Free Trade Agreement and 1992 seems bound to make British-Canadian relations less distinctive and increasingly a part of a North American-European Community relationship. Australia and New Zealand, on the other hand, are in quite a different situation. For a start, they are culturally a great deal closer to Britain than is Canada. The soap opera *Neighbours* obtained a popularity in Britain in the late 1980s that came from instant recognition of the sort of hum-drum lower middle class life portrayed; it showed the place where auntie and the cousins live. Sport also binds the Australians (and New Zealanders) closer to Britain than the Canadians, who play neither cricket nor rugby. The bicentennial bravado mentioned with distaste by Professor Millar (and others) was perhaps understandable in a country cutting the trail for its own destiny, but the backside of Asia is a lonely place for small white countries and the value of a powerful relative in a rich and expanding Europe is likely to grow rather than diminish. Australia may not want to be over-associated with Britain as it seeks to identify itself in Asian eyes as an independent nation rather than a quasi-colony, but it will not, on the other hand, want to be over-dependent on the goodwill and trade of Japan.

The Indians in Britain

The Commonwealth is a community of contrasts, and for the British the contrasts sharpen where the Old Commonwealth ends and the New begins. At that point it becomes a Commonwealth of 'them' and 'us'. To be fair, much of the Commonwealth thinks of Britain in the same way. But it is different from the them-and-us relations which obtain between developed white nations and non-white countries generally. 'If I am at a cocktail party and I see an Englishman or an Australian, or anyone else from a Commonwealth country for that matter, I will probably go up and speak to him in preference to anyone else', a black diplomat explained to the author. 'I am not quite sure why, but I think it is because there is so much more we can talk about very easily and freely. We understand one another, I suppose.' The understandings run deep (as often does the distrust) and the reasons do not stem from history alone.

The now much-abridged privileges of imperial citizenship have led to the establishment in Britain of large Commonwealth communities. A Briton does not have to go to Bombay or Barbados to meet the New Commonwealth; it is often in the same street and usually no further away than just around the corner. The Indian High Commission in London counts between 700 and 800,000 people resident in Britain as Indians, regardless of whether they are British nationals – as big a population as that boasted by many Commonwealth mini-states. If to the High Commission's figure are added the Indians who have migrated from East Africa and the Caribbean, the total is well over 1 million. The majority are Sikhs, the rest mainly Hindus. One can search for the Commonwealth component in Indian foreign policy, examine

Delhi's bilateral relations with the member states and come to the conclusion that it is these large communities of Indian emigrants in many parts of the old empire which explain why the Commonwealth is important to India.

It is not, of course, an homogenous Indian population which lives in Britain, or one that has undivided affection for Delhi. The Sikhs have imported the violent politics of religious nationalism from the Punjab. The extradition of Sikh extremists remains an unresolved issue between London and Delhi; and the antipathy between Sikhs and Hindus in Britain is considerably more intense than that between the Asian community generally (which includes a large number of Pakistani and Bangladeshi Muslims) and the white working class. All of which helps to explain why when Rajiv Gandhi meets Mrs Thatcher for talks on the margin of Commonwealth summits, the discussion focuses on the Sikhs and the Indian community in Britain and not on the British aid programme or sanctions against South Africa.

Anyone who takes a look at the Indian community in Britain is impressed by its self-reliance, its willingness to accept hardship and intolerance and the dynamism of its millionaires. If the Canadians have taken over large areas of London's Docklands, the Gujeratis have moved into the vast majority of the city's corner-shops and newsagents, the Punjabis into 60 per cent of its off-licences, the Tamils into the petrol stations, and, everywhere, there are Indian restaurants (an estimated 7,000 in Britain) and, in increasing numbers, Indian-owned homes for the elderly. The Indian shopkeepers, the middle-class professionals, doctors and lawyers, and the growing elite of millionaire businessmen are engaged in a mutual courtship with the Conservative Party, whose leading politicians from the Prime Minister down make a point of turning up at Hindu Diwali parties and similar occasions which offer high visibility. The Asians have traditionally been Labour voters, but the swing to the right was noticeable in a number of constituencies in the 1987 election. The Conservatives estimate that as many as 25 per cent voted Tory.

Indians of both right and left claim that a break-out into the mainstream of British political life is occurring, keeping pace with growing prosperity and economic influence. That, however, may not be quite the same thing as integration. The energy and application of the Indian community may strike the outsider; he also sees how enclosed it still is. The majority remain enfolded by religion, family and language, their gaze fixed backwards on the events and politics in India, the outside world around them all too often seen through a refraction of grievances, much of it provided by their press. There are a score of weekly and monthly Asian newspapers and magazines in Britain, less than half of them written in English. A reference to 'the Prime Minister' in this context refers to Gandhi, not Thatcher. British racism and the grievances which can be attributed to it are their stock-in-trade. In a typical issue of the tabloid *Asian Times*, in December 1988, all four news items on its front page were concerned with either racial violence or discrimination. The choice presumably reflected the way the readers felt about Britain.

It would be hard to imagine anyone more integrated than Mrs Shreela Flather, a leading Asian-Indian member of the Conservative Party, as she sat in her pleasant house near Maidenhead: married to an Englishman, a JP, a former mayor of Windsor and Maidenhead, a member of the Economic and Social Committee of the European Community and a host of other bodies. She described an Indian community in which the caste system was as firmly entrenched as ever, where arranged marriages were more tightly organized than in India, and where inter-marriage with whites was rare. 'If I can share a thought with you, it is that the pattern of life in India is being repeated here', she said.[5] The barriers were not exactly falling on the other side of the racial divide, either. Her application to join the Maidenhead Conservative Club went unanswered and she was told later that it was 'full up'. It is hard to imagine a Canadian or Australian applicant being treated in that manner, but they are 'us', of course, in British eyes, and Asians remain 'them', especially in the Conservative and Labour clubs, which are notorious for practising de facto segregation.

Conclusion

Would any British prime minister, even today, view with indifference a large number of resignations from the Commonwealth, whether as the result of British policy or from some other cause? Professor Dennis Austin asked in his Chatham House paper *The Commonwealth and Britain*. He suspected that, despite a falling off of public interest and the government's coolness towards the Secretariat, Britain was more concerned about the Commonwealth and its future than were other member countries.

Mrs Thatcher's attitude towards the Commonwealth has been ambivalent – an unusual attitude for her. It arouses no enthusiasm, but she does not want it to fall apart, a development which would lead to her being accused of casting away Britain's inheritance through neglect and narrowness of vision. She has not produced any ideas for changing it from a moribund into a vital organization and it is not clear whether the ideas she does have amount to much more than turning it into a saluting base from which a respectful assembly can be reviewed every two years. However, even that would require a few incentives to persuade the troops to turn up.

The Foreign Secretary's speech in 1986 on the theme of 'The Commonwealth: Who Cares?' provides little in the way of enlightenment about government thoughts on the subject, other than a belief that the organization is a 'force for good in the world' and that its meetings should not be devalued. Equally revealing has been the negative attitude of the Commons' Foreign Affairs Select Committee, which has been totally unreceptive in the past few years to proposals that it should hold hearings on the Commonwealth or any aspect of it. In the shaping of foreign policy the Commonwealth's influence is marginal, of little more importance to Britain than it is to, say, India, whose only departure from a policy of non-alignment has been its treaty of friendship and co-operation with the Soviet Union. Which is not to say that it has no importance as a platform or as a useful, undemanding link with a variety of other countries that have a language and a part of their history in common. That is where the Commonwealth still counts.

There is, perhaps, a pointer to the way the British Government would like things to go in its interest in French management of *La Francophonie*. 'We are learning from the French in a practical sense', was the opinion of Lynda Chalker, Minister of State at the Foreign office.[6] One can understand the reasons for the interest: an organization which steered away from political rows over South Africa and concentrated on matters like education, the English language, environmental problems and, above all, economic relations between the Third World and the industrial nations would still have plenty of contentious issues to add zest to its summits and might in time find its pronouncements carrying more weight than do those of the present-day Commonwealth.

The Kuala Lumpur summit in October 1989 is likely to see the Commonwealth moving towards the peak of its membership – 50 States, with the possibility of 51 at some future stage if Fiji is ever readmitted. India has dropped its opposition to Pakistan rejoining since the restoration of democracy and the meeting in early 1989 between Rajiv Gandhi and Benazir Bhutto. In fact, it would be prepared to sponsor Pakistan's membership,[7] a step that would have the support of the summit's host, Malaysia, an Islamic country like Pakistan. The other potential member is Namibia, whose independence will justifiably be regarded by the British Government as evidence that the policy of constructive engagement with Pretoria is working. But an exhausted acceptance by the African and other Commonwealth countries that Mrs Thatcher's policy has its merits (and is, in any case, unchangeable) and that the sanctions issue should be allowed to subside would not necessarily carry with it a willingness to redirect energies towards other issues and new approaches. Even with sanctions on the front burner, neither the current military leader of Africa's most important and populous State, Nigeria, nor the leader of its neighbour Ghana has so far found the time to attend a Commonwealth summit; with sanctions and South Africa shoved to the back, they and others might find even less reason to attend. There has always been lurking in the wings of Commonwealth summits the question 'What are we going to talk about when South Africa is no longer an issue?'

The Commonwealth, it should be remembered, is barred by its rules from discussing its member states' internal problems, unless, of course, they want them tabled. The problems of divided Cyprus are regularly discussed at the request of its government, but those of Sri Lanka, where Indian troops fight Tamil insurrectionaries, are not. If one looks through the summit declarations after Singapore in 1971 (when president Milton Obote of Uganda was overthrown by a coup) one will find lengthy references to South Africa and Rhodesia but nothing at all about Idi Amin's atrocities in Uganda. No one stands up to denounce military government in Nigeria or Ghana. Search through the 1973 summit communiqué and you will find that new Commonwealth member Bangladesh is welcomed, but there is no mention of the 1972 resignation of Pakistan, whose military defeat by India led to Bangladesh's independence. Matters of that nature are not aired at the summits. Nor are human rights problems affecting member states. If they were, the Commonwealth would soon fall apart.

So what can the Commonwealth usefully discuss apart from South Africa? The dire poverty of some of its members? Bangladesh, for example? India? Some of the African or the mini-states? Poverty is, of course, regularly discussed and Shridath Ramphal played a leading role in promoting the New International Economic Order, but the Commonwealth is not in itself an important conduit for aid. As we have seen, the two richest members, Britain and Canada, favour Commonwealth countries in their bilateral aid programmes, but do not spend very much money on the Commonwealth Fund for Technical Co-operation. Their multilateral aid goes through the international financial institutions, such as the International Monetary Fund and the World Bank, and, in Britain's case, the European Community. The Commonwealth is a homely forum where rich and poor states speaking the same language can meet and exchange views and, on many issues, reach a consensus, but it cannot be said to be an effective pressure group or to be noticeably useful in an institutional sense as a problem-solver or a means of bringing about change. Hard logic drives one towards the view that its condition is terminal, but logic is not necessarily a good guide when dealing with bodies like the Commonwealth which

retain a considerable amount of affection and, partly because
of that, have the potential for constructive activity in some
fields. Three obvious ones suggest themselves: the relations
between rich and poor countries, with a special emphasis on
the approaching Year of Europe, 1992; the mini-states; and
climatic change and its impact on the number of Commonwealth countries.

North-South. Malcolm Fraser was the president of a conference just outside London in mid-1988 entitled 'Building on
Commonwealth Links' (see Chapter 2). Afterwards he cir-
culated his opening address. It reads like the keynote speech
for an election campaign, and since he is in the running for
the Commonwealth's secretary-generalship, perhaps it should
be regarded as just that. It is interesting largely for the
emphasis it places on the positive side of Britain's membership of the European Community. Britain matters more to the
Community because of the Commonwealth; equally, Britain,
as a significant economic power, provides an important
linkage for other members of the Commonwealth to the
Community and other major states. The more actively Britain
plays its role within the Community, the more effectively it
will be able to contribute to Commonwealth affairs.

A re-orientation of the Commonwealth along these lines
might restore to it a degree of economic reality. The
Commonwealth would in no way detract from Britain's full
commitment to the Community; it would enhance its position.
Within the Community itself, there would be increasing scope
for co-operation between Britain and France, and with other
ex-colonial powers, on the problems and interests of the
components of their old empires, developed as well as under-
developed countries. If national rivalries within the Community do not get in the way, there could eventually be a
convergence of ex-colonial organizations centred on Brussels,
where the ACP countries have a permanent delegation.

Mini-states. These diminutive, often unviable, states form,
as we have seen, the larger part of the Commonwealth's
membership, and they are one of its unique features. It
provides them with a collective platform and an informal,

easily accessible network of helpers that exists nowhere else. If, for example, an official in a small island government in the Pacific needs help in drafting a bill the easiest and quickest way of obtaining it is usually to call the appropriate department in Canberra or Wellington. Support for the Commonwealth is probably stronger among the mini-states than anywhere else. A leaf might be taken from the Commonwealth Parliamentary Association's book by holding a short summit of mini-state leaders immediately before the main summit. Equally worth examining is the idea of the creation of a small states bureau within the Secretariat, possibly with regional representation.

Climatic change. This is an increasingly important world problem. And one of its aspects – rising sea levels – poses a direct threat to the survival beyond the first half of the next century of several Commonwealth countries, notably Bangladesh, the Maldives, Tuvalu and Kiribati. Mrs Thatcher gave the Commonwealth a push in the direction of greater concentration on this problem when she ensured that two of the three sessions of the March 1989 ozone layer conference in London were chaired by Commonwealth figures, Geoffrey Palmer, the New Zealand Deputy Prime Minister, and Sonny Ramphal. Brian Mulroney, the Canadian Prime Minister, and Eddie Fenech-Adami, the Maltese Prime Minister, have taken the lead in promoting a 'law of the atmosphere' charter in the United Nations. The Commonwealth Secretariat has been engaged in a study of climatic change since the issue was raised at the Vancouver summit.

What the heads of government need to do at Kuala Lumpur is to take stock and define in a realistic way where the Commonwealth has been useful in the past and what it can usefully do in the future. The 1985–7 summits, for all their trauma, at least demonstrated what it cannot do, namely organize concerted political-economic action. That in turn demonstrated, admittedly in a rather negative way, a sometimes neglected truth about the Commonwealth: that Britain remains the pivotal nation. Nothing is going to work unless the British Government is committed to seeing that it does.

And beyond the government lies public opinion, which has to be persuaded that the Commonwealth is worth preserving. Mrs Thatcher's Government has not been notable for promoting the idea that the Commonwealth is of value. In fact, its presentation of its position at recent summits and its general neglect of the organization have tended to lower still further the limited public esteem in which it is held. Only a government lead can begin to change that; and the lead, of course, will depend not on a sudden rush of sentiment, but on the Commonwealth being turned into a body that is seen to be doing valuable work. Equally, it is up to the New Commonwealth countries to show that they are sufficiently interested in the organization to want to give it a new impetus. Britain and the Old Commonwealth countries give the impression that they want to see evidence of that before they make up their minds on the vexed problem of 'Where next?'

As a refreshing change from the dominance of southern African issues, the Kuala Lumpur summit will turn attention to Asia and in particular will mark the return of Malaysia to active participation in Commonwealth affairs. Its Prime Minister, Dr Mahathir Mohamad, has been rather dismissive in the past. Singapore's Lee Kuan Yew shows a distant interest in an organization which too often tests his patience, but makes his presence felt occasionally at summits. Sri Lanka is too tied up in its internal affairs to bother much about anything else. Bangladesh's desperate poverty casts it on the world's charity rather than that of the Commonealth alone. Which leaves India, a commonwealth on its own, as it was an empire on its own before 1947. The Commonwealth is part of the platform for India's stance as a Third World leader, and is therefore regarded as useful. If the Indians can be persuaded to undertake some positive thinking about the Commonwealth's future, then some of the other 'new' members might engage in the same process. What is certain is that few of them want to see the institution disappear. Its familiarity, and the friendships which have grown with it, make it useful as a meeting place and one which, its supporters argue, is a great deal more congenial as a forum than the United Nations. Moreover, from a more hard-headed point of view, the connection with a Britain committed to ensuring that the European Community's post-1992 economic defences do not endanger their interests would make securing the survival of the Commonwealth a worthwhile exercise.

The use of Britain's position in the Community to provide a new centre of gravity for the Commonwealth would certainly have consequences for the Secretariat. For a start, it would make the Commonwealth more clearly Anglocentric. And that could be part of an argument for trimming the Secretariat into a leaner organization geared to doing a few things well in the fields mentioned above and in one of its most recent ventures, distance learning, a partnership between Commonwealth centres of higher education employing satellites and radio. Many of its other activities (the Women and Development Programme and some of the other human resource programmes, for example) could be carried on quite satisfactorily through a strengthened network of non-governmental organizations on the lines already being pursued, notably by the Commonwealth Trust, aka the Royal Commonwealth Society.

But is that the sort of Commonwealth which a highly-charged political secretary-general like Fraser would want to steer? And, equally relevant, would Britain want a secretary-general on the Fraser lines? And who, of course, do the Africans want to see in the post? These are questions – as much a matter of approach as of personality – which will have to be thrashed out at the Kuala Lumpur summit. The appointment will be an important one since it will set the political level at which the future Commonwealth will work.

As with all organizations, it is necessary to accept the limitations. The Commonwealth may grow slightly in numbers, but it is unlikely to increase in importance. It may be overtaken by overlapping bodies of more relevance to the members and dwindle still further in significance as well as attraction. One of the striking developments in the contemporary Commonwealth is how rapidly much of it is becoming more widely internationalized, slipping out of a purely Commonwealth definition into something larger which allows more opportunities. This may weaken the organization, but it is not necessarily a fatal trend provided that the areas where it can operate effectively are identified and it is given the means and encouragement to do so.

And here we return to the key question of the importance Britain attaches to the Commonwealth. It took two decades for Britain to decide against the instincts and traditions which made the Commonwealth such a powerful emotional force (and handicap) and recast its policy in the direction of Europe and economic reality. And even now that yearning for the wider spaces makes itself felt in the limitations placed on Britain's involvement. The Commonwealth is part of that wider world which becomes more attractive to British politicians when the demands of Europe grow more exacting. There is every reason to think that it provides a foothold outside 'Fortress Europe' which successive British Governments will hope to maintain.

British policy is inevitably, and rightly, protective of British interests and a Conservative Government's perceptions of what they are do not differ fundamentally from those of its Labour predecessors. Whatever the tensions caused by the clashes over South Africa, frustration is a bad counsellor and patience, usually, a good one. The patience underlying Britain's traditional approach to the Commonwealth can be interpreted as akin to wisdom. The Commonwealth is not a contract between its members, but it is a bond. For Britain, the key member, it is a remarkably complex bond composed of strands of obligation, sentiment, prestige and the more solid interest that all important industrial powers have in keeping their ties with the world's poorer nations vital and constantly renewed. It would be a miserable rejection of a proud, and honourable, tradition – unmatched by any other imperial nation – if Britain were to allow the Commonwealth to die through neglect, hostility, or just plain lack of imagination.

Notes

Chapter one Transition to the New Commonwealth

1. Final communiqué, Commonwealth prime ministers' meeting, London, 26 April 1949.
2. Attlee to Nehru, 20 March 1949, CAB 127/3741.
3. Constituent Assembly, Delhi, 16 May 1949.
4. Robert Menzies, *Afternoon Light* (London: Cassell, 1967), p. 230. See Chapter 10 for Menzies' views on the Crown and the Commonwealth.
5. In a conversation with the author, Melbourne, October 1981.
6. Joe (later Lord) Garner, *The Commonwealth Office* (London: Heinemann, 1978), p. 340.
7. Ibid., p. 347.
8. Arnold Smith with Clyde Sanger, *Stitches in Time* (London: André Deutsch, 1981), p. 10.
9. Garner, *The Commonwealth Office*, p. 351.
10. Interview with the author, June, 1988.
11. See Smith, *Stitches in Time*, for this and other episodes in his time as Secretary-General.
12. J. F. B. Miller, *Survey of Commonwealth Affairs: Problems of Expansion and Attrition, 1953–69* (Oxford: Oxford University Press for the Royal Institute of International Affairs, 1974), p. 123.

Chapter two Ramphal's Secretariat

1. *The Times* (of London) profile, 17 November 1983.
2. Interview with the author, June 1988.
3. Ibid.
4. *Reflect on Things Past: The Memoirs of Lord Carrington* (London: Collins, 1988). See chapter 13 on Rhodesia.
5. Shridath Ramphal, Annual conference of the International Defence and Aid Fund for Southern Africa, 10 May 1985.
6. Dennis Austin, *The Commonwealth and Britain* (London: Royal Institute of International Affairs, 1988), Chatham House Paper No. 41.
7. Introduction to the 1985 report of the Commonwealth Secretary-General.
8. June 1988 interview with the author. In 1975–6 the Secretariat had a budget of £1,622,735 with a staff of 210. By 1987–8 the budget had grown to £6,543,515 and the staff to 232. Another senior Commonwealth source gives the 1988 staff figure as 271, a 29 per cent increase. However, other Commonwealth sources say the missing 39 properly belong to the CFTC. During the same period the CFTC budget rose from £5.5m. to £22m.
9. 'Building on Commonwealth Links', held at St Catherine's Foundation, Windsor, in June 1988.
10. Arthur Kilgore and James Mayall, 'Economic Cooperation' in A. J. R. Groom and Paul Taylor (eds), *The Commonwealth in the 1980s: Challenges and Opportunities* (London: Macmillan, 1984), p 152.
11. Philip Ayres, *Malcolm Fraser* (Melbourne: Heinemann, 1987), p. 348.
12. Alan Renouf, *Malcolm Fraser and Australian Foreign Policy* (Sydney: Australian Professional Publications, 1986), pp. 135–6.

Chapter three From Empire to Commonwealth

1. Nicholas Mansergh, *The Commonwealth Experience* (London: Weidenfeld and Nicolson, 1969), p. 19.
2. John Arthur Roebuck, *The Colonies of England: A Plan for a Government of Some Portion of Our Colonial Possessions* (London, 1849).
3. Stuart J. Reid, *Life and Letters of the First Earl of Durham*, 2 vols (London, 1906). See also Leonard Cooper, *Radical Jack* (London: Cresset Press, 1959).
4. John Buchan, *Memory Hold the Door* (London: Hodder and Stoughton, 1940).
5. Letter to Lord Derby, 30 September 1866.

6   C. A. Bodelsen, *Studies in Mid-Victorian Imperialism* (Copenhagen, 1924), p. 79.

Chapter four The South African matrix: ideals and magnanimity

1   Charles Wentworth Dilke, *Greater Britain: A Record of Travel in English-Speaking Countries during 1866 and 1867* (London, 1868) 2 vols.
2   See chapter on Seeley in Bodelsen, *Studies in Mid-Victorian Imperialism*.
3   John Seeley, *The Expansion of England* (London, 1883), p. 184, 1909 edn.
4   Quoted in Waldo Hilary Dunn, *James Anthony Froude* (London: Oxford University Press, 1963), vol. 2, p. 352.
5   Ibid., p. 407.
6   Letter quoted in Thomas Pakenham, *The Boer War* (London: Weidenfeld and Nicolson, 1979), p. 488.
7   Buchan, *Memory Hold the Door*, p. 102.
8   For more detailed explanations of British attitudes see Pakenham, *The Boer War* and Ronald Robinson and John Gallagher with Alice Denny, *Africa and the Victorians: The Official Mind of Imperialism* (London: Macmillan, 1965). Material in this and the following paragraph is largely drawn from these two works.
9   V. O. Mahajan, *The Nationalist Movement in India* (Delhi: Sterling Publishers, 1979), p. 131.
10 For Curtis's ideas see his *Civitas Dei* (London, 1934) and *The Problem of the Commonwealth* (London, 1916); also L. S. Amery, *Political Life* (London: Hutchinson, 1953–5) vol. 1, p. 178.
11 Lord Elton, *Imperial Commonwealth* (London: Collins, 1945), p. 445.
12 *The Political Future of the British Commonwealth and Empire* (London: Royal Empire Society, 1945).
13 For a survey of inter-war Commonwealth history see Denis Judd and Peter Slinn, *The Evolution of the Modern Commonwealth, 1902–80* (London: Macmillan, 1982).
14 Mansergh, *Commonwealth Experience*, pp. 237–8.
15 Robert Grant Irving, *Indian Summer* (New Haven: Yale University Press, 1981), p. 162.
16 George Lansbury, *Labour's Way with the Commonwealth* (London: 'Labour Shows the Way' series, 1935).
17 Fenner Brockway, *African Socialism* (London: The Bodley Head, 1963).

18 Doc. 20 in Roger Bullen and M. E. Pelly (eds), *Documents on British Policy Overseas: The London Conference, Anglo-American Relations and Cold War Strategy*, series 2, vol. 2, Jan–June 1950 (London: HMSO, 1987).
19 11 January 1952. Quoted in Miller, *Survey of Commonwealth Affairs*.

Chapter five   Nassau: the first of a trilogy of troubled summits

1 *The Commonwealth at the Summit: Communiqués of Commonwealth Heads of Government meetings 1944–1986*. (London: Commonwealth Secretariat, 1987).
2 Private communication to the author.
3 *The Sunday Times*, 12 May 1988.
4 Estimate by Sir Geoffrey Howe in speech to Royal Commonwealth Society, 17 May 1988.
5 *Annual Abstract of Statistics* (London: HMSO, 1988 edition).
6 *Census of Overseas Assets; MO4; 1984* (London: HMSO, 1984).

Chapter six   Through Pretoria to Vancouver

1 Article by Professor Hermann Giliomee in *The Cape Times*, 2 May 1986.
2 Kenneth Kaunda, *Kaunda on Violence* (London: Collins, 1980), p. 164.
3 *Globe and Mail* (Toronto) 7 August 1986.
4 *British Aid to Southern Africa: a Force for Peaceful Change and Development* (London: HMSO, 1987).
5 The SADCC member countries are: Angola, Botswana, Lesotho, Malawi, Mozambique, Swaziland, Tanzania, Zambia and Zimbabwe.
6 *Globe and Mail* (Toronto) 13 October 1987.
7 The Canadians, in particular, were sensitive to the way in which British newspapers covered the summit. A study of them shows that quality papers were reasonably dispassionate, but the tabloids took a juicier approach (with the exception of *The Mirror*). *The Sun* had Kaunda and other black leaders launching a 'torrent of abuse' against Thatcher (13 October 1987) and Thatcher and Mulroney engaged in a 'massive row'. *The Daily Express* quoted Ramphal as suggesting that Canada should take over the leadership of the Commonwealth from Britain (13 October) and depicted Mulroney as having a 'blazing row'

with Thatcher behind closed doors (14 Ocotber). It was the 'Maggie poised for victory in sanctions war' note at the conclusion of the summit which convinced the Canadians, and others, that the coverage had been orchestrated for political reasons.
8 *The Independent* 9 February, 1989.

Chapter seven The politics of aid

1 Interview with Kaunda in the September–October 1988 issue of *The Courier*, published by the European Community.
2 *British Overseas Aid, 1987* and *British Aid Statistics, 1983–1987*, both published by the Overseas Development Administration.
3 *British Overseas Aid, 1987*.
4 *Observations by the Government on the Foreign Affairs Select Committee report Bilateral Aid: Country Programmes.* October 1987 (London: HMSO).
5 Para 25, *Foreign Affairs Select Committee report on FCO/ODA Expenditure, 1988–89*. July 1988 (London: HMSO).
6 European File October 1987 entitled *The European Community and the Third World* (Brussels: Commission of the European Communities).
7 Richard Gwyn, *The 49th Paradox: Canada in North America* (Toronto: McLelland and Stewart, 1985).
8 Of Commonwealth inspiration; founded in 1950 with the aim of countering communist encroachment in Asia. It has an office in Colombo and appears in the list of official Commonwealth organizations, but in fact is an early example of the Commonwealth trend towards internationalization. It has grown from the original seven Commonwealth countries into a membership of 26 nations, the majority of which are non-Commonwealth. Japan is the largest donor, providing twice as much as the next largest, the United States (Source: *The Statesman's Year Book, 1988–89*). It was under the Plan that Canada provided India with a nuclear research reactor which the Indians diverted to producing the material for their 1974 bomb test explosion.
9 Peter C. Dobell, *Canada's Search for New Roles: Foreign Policy in the Trudeau Era* (London: Oxford University Press for the Royal Institute of International Affairs, 1972), p. 123.
10 Ibid., p. 125.
11 Michael Tucker, *International Perspectives in Canadian Foreign Policy* (May/June 1973 edn) (Toronto, 1980).
12 Report by Xavier Deniau of the Foreign Affairs Committee to

the French National Assembly, June 1970.

Chapter eight   The international monarchy

1. *The Times*, 20 October 1969, quoted in Elizabeth Longford, *Elizabeth R* (London: Weidenfeld and Nicolson, 1983).
2. George Winterton, *Monarchy to Republic: Australian Republican Government* (Melbourne: Oxford University Press, 1986).
3. Interviewed by author, November 1988.
4. *Sydney Morning Herald*, 9 October 1987.
5. A. Berriedale Keith, *The King and the Imperial Crown* (London, 1936), p. 452.
6. Thames Television, London, interview, 22 April 1986.
7. J. W. Wheeler-Bennett, *King George VI* (London: Macmillan, 1958).
8. The King's Diary, 28 October 1943, quoted in Wheeler-Bennett, *King George VI*.
9. See Sidney Lee's biography, *King Edward VII*, vol. 1 (London, 1925).
10. Dilke, *Greater Britain*.
11. Quoted from Sidney Lee, *Queen Victoria* (London, 1902).
12. Quoted in Frank Hardie, *The Political Influence of Queen Victoria* (London, 1935).
13. André Maurois, *Disraeli* (London, 1927), p. 266.

Chapter nine   The institutions: crumbling edifices, changing uses

1. Interview with the author, October 1988.
2. On 13 April 1988. Fourth Report of the House of Commons Foreign Affairs Committee, session 1987–88.
3. Interviews with Prof. Millar and Sir Zelman Cowen in November, 1988.
4. From description of CPA in *Vacher's Parliamentary Companion*.

Chapter ten   The sporting commonwealth

1. Quoted in Ayres, *Malcolm Fraser*. The octogenarian Bradman was due to visit South Africa in mid-1989, having accepted an invitation to attend the centenary celebrations of South African Test cricket.

2 See *Emburey*, the autobiography of John Emburey (London, Partridge Press, 1987).
3 See *Daily Telegraph* 10 September 1988.
4 Gondwanaland: the name given by geologists to the landmass which millions of years ago joined Africa, Antarctica and South America in one continent. A South African rugby team toured Chile in the last quarter of 1988, but was stopped from touring Argentina. The same team was believed by SAN-ROC to have gone the long way home via London in November to watch the England-Australia rugby Test, when it slipped under the anti-apartheid net to play a secret game against a scratch side at Maidenhead.

Chapter eleven The mega-problems of mini-states

1 *Vulnerability: Small States in the Global Society*. Report of a Commonwealth Consultative Group (London: Commonwealth Secretariat, 1985).
2 Ibid., p. 93.
3 Military and paramilitary forces in the Commonwealth Caribbean are negligible in size and probably in quality. *The Military Balance, 1988-89* (published by the International Institute for Strategic Studies, London), lists 600 coastguards in the Bahamas; a force of 650 soldiers in Belize; 2,200 soldiers and 150 coastguards in Jamaica; 2,750 troops and 600 coastguards in Trinidad and Tobago. Guyana, on the South American mainland, has more substantial forces: 5,450 men all told.
4 Interviewed by the author, November 1988.
5 *Caribbean Insight*, July, 1988.
6 *Latin American and Caribbean Review, 1988*.
7 *The Caribbean Handbook, 1988*.
8 See Wiliams's *From Columbus to Castro: The History of the Caribbean 1492-1969* (London: Andre Deutsch, 1970). Also Anthony Payne, *The Politics of the Caribbean Community, 1961-79* (Manchester University Press, 1980), p. 19: 'The fate of the Federation was conclusively settled by its inability to become anything more than a forum for the expression of regional rivalries. It had always been seen in the West Indies as a means to an end, latterly as the gateway to independence, and never, therefore, as an end and an ideal in its own right.'
9 Seminar at Commonwealth Institute 12 November 1988, organized by Eastern Caribbean High Commission, Grenada High Commission and the Dominica Consulate.

10 See *Ageing Minorities* (London: Commission for Racial Equality, 1987).
11 *Commonwealth Year Book, 1987* (London: HMSO).

Chapter twelve   The Commonwealth and Britain

1 Figures from *Australia News*, 28 October 1988, and the Australian High Commission respectively.
2 *ABS. Foreign investment 1986–87*. On an annual basis, Japanese investment has probably been ahead of the British and Americans during the past few years.
3 Interview with author, November 1988.
4 See the chapter on the Commonwealth by David McIntrye in John Henderson, Keith Jackson and Richard Kennaway (eds), *Beyond New Zealand: The Foreign Policy of a Small State* (Auckland: Methuen, 1980).
5 Interview with author, January 1989.
6 Interview with author, October 1988.
7 Indian Ministry of External Affairs statement, January 1989.

Commonwealth Members

Independent States

Country	Population	Government and date of joining	
Antigua and Barbuda	77,000	M	1981
Australia	15,170,000	M	1931*
Bahamas	218,000	M	1973
Bangladesh	92,859,000	R	1972
Barbados	251,000	M	1966
Belize	150,000	M	1981
Botswana	966,000	R	1966
Britain	56,280,000	M	
Brunei	233,000	NM	1984
Canada	25,923,000	M	1931*
Cyprus	645,000	R	1961
Dominica	80,000	R	1978
Gambia	682,000	R	1965
Ghana	12,169,000	R	1957
Grenada	113,000	M	1974
Guyana	798,000	R	1966
India	716,985,000	R	1947
Jamaica	2,246,000	M	1962
Kenya	18,115,000	R	1963
Kiribati	60,000	R	1979
Lesotho	1,404,000	NM	1966
Malawi	6,452,000	R	1964

Country	Population	Government and date of joining	
Malaysia	14,529,000	NM	1957
Maldives	163,000	R	1982
Malta	360,000	R	1964
Mauritius	985,000	M	1968
Nauru	8,000	R	1968
New Zealand	3,160,000	M	1931*
Nigeria	90,572,000	R	1960
Papua New Guinea	3,128,000	M	1975
St Christopher–Nevis	53,000	M	1983
St Lucia	126,000	M	1979
St Vincent/Grenadines	101,000	M	1979
Seychelles	64,000	R	1976
Sierra Leone	3,194,000	R	1961
Singapore	2,471,000	R	1965
Solomon Islands	245,000	M	1978
Sri Lanka	15,189,000	R	1948
Swaziland	664,000	NM	1968
Tanzania	19,763,000	R	1961
Trinidad/Tobago	1,129,000	R	1962
Tuvalu	8,000	M	1978
Uganda	13,451,000	R	1962
Vanuatu	123,000	R	1980
Western Samoa	159,000	R	1970
Zambia	6,045,000	R	1964
Zimbabwe	7,499,000	R	1980

M Monarchy–Queen Elizabeth   NM National monarchy
R Republic; * Statute of Westminster.
(Source: Dept. of External Affairs, Ottawa).

Associated states and departments

UK

	Population
Anguilla	7,000
Bermuda	79,000

	Population
Brit. Virgin Islands	13,000
Cayman Islands	20,000
Falkland Islands	2,000
Gibraltar	29,000
Hong Kong	5,500,000
Montserrat	12,000
Pitcairn Islands	67
St Helena	6,000 ·
Turks and Caicos Is.	10,000

AUSTRALIA

Christmas Island	3,000
Cocos Islands	600
Norfolk Island	2,000

NEW ZEALAND

Cook Islands	23,000
Niue	2,000
Tokelau	2,000

Index

Able, Sir Frederick, 120
ACP states, 94–6 *passim*, 154, 157, 171 *see also individual countries*
Africa, 10–12, 16, 17, 20, 31, 45, 58–9, 60, 65, 68–9, 73, 74, 79, 82, 83, 88–90 *passim* 97, 99–101 *passim*, 110, 132, 135, 136, 139, 142, 147, 169, 174 *see also individual countries*
  South-West, 50
  Southern – Development Co-ordination Conference, 83–4, 93
  UN Special Session on, 90
African National Congress, 70, 71, 74, 75, 88, 143–4
African Socialism, 58
agreements
  ACCT, 100
  imperial preference, 55
  Gleneagles (1977), 67, 134, 140–1
  US-Canada (1923), 55; (1988), 97, 105, 156, 161, 164
  tripartite on Namibia, 94
agriculture, 99, 125
Agence de Coopération Culturelle et Technique (ACCT), 98–100 *passim*
aid, 29, 30, 69, 83, 84, 89–103, 156, 157, 166, 170; tied, 92
AIDS, 90
Albert, Prince, 113–14 *passim*
Alfred, Prince, 114
All Blacks, 20, 139, 140, 143
alumina, 157

Alva, Margaret, 135, 138
Amery, Julian, 131; L. S., 52, 54
Amin, Idi, 65, 139, 170
American Revolution, 34, 37
Angola, 83, 93
Antigua, 155
Anyaoku, Chief Emeka, 32
ANZUS pact, 56, 163
Argentina, 143, 183n4
arms sales, 81, 133, 140
Armstrong, Sir Robert, 70
Asia, 11, 96, 156, 165–7 *passim*, 173 *see also individual countries*
Asian Times, 167
Asquith, H. H., 49
Attlee, Clement, 7, 58
Austin, Dennis, 27, 168
Australia/Australians, 2, 6, 8, 13, 27, 29, 30, 32, 37, 51, 54–6 *passim*, 68, 71, 85, 106–7, 112, 122–3, 126–7, 133, 149, 153, 154, 159, 161–5
  Studies Centre, 127, 162
Austria, 92, 96

Babangida, Maj.-Gen. Ibrahim, 32
Bahamas, 66, 71, 152, 183n3
Baker, Sir Herbert, 5, 57, 80, 128
bananas, 95, 155–7 *passim*
Bangladesh, 28, 166, 170, 172, 173
Banda, Dr, 142
Barbados, 95, 151
Barber, Lord, 73
Barrow, Dame Nita, 73
bauxite, 155, 157

Bavadra, Dr, 109
BDEEP, 127
Beaverbrook, Lord, 160–1
Bechuanaland, 50
beef, 95
Beira corridor, 93
Belgium, 99
Belize, 1, 151, 154, 183n3
Bentham, Jeremy, 37
Berriedale Keith, A., 108
Bhutto, Benazir, 169
Bishop, Maurice, 66, 109, 147–9 *passim*
Black, Conrad, 160–1
Bloch, Dora, 65
Bodelsen, C.A., 44
Boers, 47–53 *passim*
Boesak, Allan, 87
Bond, Alan, 162, 163
Botha, Louis, 52
Botha, President P. W., 74–80 *passim* 86, 88, 94, 143
Botha, 'Pik', 74
Botswana, 24, 76, 95, 142
Bourne, Richard, 122
Boycott, Geoffrey, 134
Bradman, Don, 133, 182n1
Brandt Commission, 28
Briggs, Lord, 28
Britain, 1–4 *passim*, 6, 9, 10, 12, 13, 16, 19, 21–7, 29, 30, 34–60 *passim*, 65, 68, 71, 72, 75–84, 86–9, 91–3, 95, 100, 102–3, 109, 117–35 *passim*, 141, 142, 147–9, 151–2, 154, 156, 157, 159–7
 and Australia, 159, 161–5
 and Canada, 38–43, 159–61, 164–5
 and New Zealand, 159, 163–5 *passim*
 and South Africa, 65–72, 75–83, 87
 aid, 91–3, 102
 Indians in, 165–7
 West Indians in, 155, 156
British North America Act, 43
Brockway, Fenner, 58
Brougham, Lord, 39, 41
Buchan, John, 40, 49
Buchanan, President, 114, 115
Budd, Zola, 142
Buller, Charles, 38, 42
Burundi, 99

Canada/Canadians, 2, 3, 6, 12–13, 18, 27, 29, 30, 38–43, 45, 51, 54–6, 65, 71, 82, 85–7, 89, 96–9, 104–6, 113–15, 133, 137–8, 152, 154, 159–61, 164, 170, 180n7, 181n8
 French, 39, 42, 98 *see also* Quebec
Caribbean, 65–6, 94–6 *passim*, 147–57 *see also individual countries*
 Organization of East – States, 151, 155–6
Canning, Lord, 116
Carlyle, Thomas, 44
Carnarvon, Lord, 47
Carrington, Lord, 18, 21, 22
Cayman Islands, 131, 153
Central African Federation, 10
Ceylon, 56
Chalker, Lynda, 123, 169
Chamberlain, Neville, 55, 86
Charles, Eugenia, 147
Charles, Prince, 8, 26, 80, 108, 109, 111–13, 118
chemicals, 157
Chile, 143, 183n4
China, 102
Christmas broadcasts, 111
Churchill, Winston, 1, 6, 55, 56, 58, 86, 113
Civitas Dei, 52–3
Clark, Joe, 84, 87
climatic change, 28, 172
Collcutt, T. E., 119
Colombo Plan, 96, 181n8
Colonial Reformers, 35, 37
Colonial Society, 128
Commonwealth
 Advisory Aeronautical Research Council, 124
 Agricultural Bureaux/CAB International, 125–6
 Air Transport Council, 124
 Consultative Group on small states, 146, 150
 Co-ordination Department, 13
 Defence Science Organization, 124
 Development Corporation, 101–2
 Directory, 124–5
 Foundation, 130
 Fund for Technical Co-operation, 27–30, 170

INDEX

Games, 79, 135–42, 144
House, 127–9 *passim*
Institute, 2, 111, 121–4
Liaison Units, 129, 130
Office, 10, 13, 15
Parliamentary Association, 130–2, 172
Place, 121–2
Press Union, 67, 124–5
Secretariat *see* Secretariat, Commonwealth
Telecommunication Organization, 124
Trust, 128–30 *passim*, 174
University, 28
Commonwealth Information, 23
conferences
  colonial (1887), 54
  Commonwealth Parliamentary, 83, 131, 172
  Imperial (1907), 51; (1917), 54, 55
  Lancaster House, 21–2, 77
  Round Table, 58
Consolidated Goldfields, 87
Cook, Geoff, 134
Cowen, Sir Zelman, 106–7, 127, 129
Cowley, Annette, 142
Craven, Danie, 143
cricket, 133–5, 164
Crosland, Anthony, 65
Crown, 8–9, 106, 108–9, 110, 116–18
  see also monarchy
Crown Agents, 102
Cuba, 93, 94, 147
de Cuellar, Perez, 18
culture, 99–101, 164
Curtis, Lionel, 51–3, 54, 58
Cyprus, 170

debt, 91
Declarations
  Gleneagles, (1977), 139–41
  Goa (1983), 62
  Melbourne (1981), 62, 141
  Nassau (1985), 62
  Singapore (1971), 140
  Vancouver (1987), 62
decolonization, 3, 58–9, 88, 100
defence, 53, 54
  Imperial – Committee, 56
Derby, Lord, 35, 116

Development Assistance Committee, 92
Dilke, Charles, 44, 46, 115
disinvestment, 68
Disraeli, Benjamin, 36, 43, 44, 50, 116, 117
Dixon, David, 138
Dobell, Peter, 98
D'Oliveira, Basil, 135
Dominica, 147, 154, 156
Douglas-Home, Sir Alec, 12, 69
drugs, 66–7, 151–3, 156
Dubois, W.E.B., 11
Duchess of York, 129
Dufferin, Lord, 51
Duncan, Sandy, 136–9 *passim*
Duncombe, Tommy, 40
Durant, Tony, 131
Durham, Lord, 38–43, 50, 57
  Report, 37–9 *passim* 42, 43

Eden, Anthony, 59
education, 24, 28, 29, 84, 100, 169, 174
Edward VII (as Prince of Wales), 5, 112–15 *passim*, 120
Egypt, 99
Elliott, John, 162
Elton, Lord, 52
Elizabeth II, Queen, 6, 23, 62, 63, 80, 104–12 *passim*, 117, 118, 124, 129
Emburey, John, 133–5 *passim*
Eminent Persons Group, 31, 70, 71, 73–6
energy, 99
English language, 1, 96, 101, 105, 133, 136, 159, 170
environment, 28, 169, 172
Ethiopia, 91
Europe, 2, 6, 7, 59, 113
  Year of, 2, 4
European Community, 2, 3, 9, 30, 55, 59, 60, 66, 71, 72, 75–6, 81, 82, 88, 91, 94–6, 99, 106, 156, 157, 161, 163–5 *passim*, 170, 171, 174, 175
Expansion of England, The, 47

Falklands, 137, 153
Fenech-Adami, Paddie, 172
Festival of Empire (1911), 136

INDEX

Fiji, 85, 87–8, 95, 109–10, 149, 169
Flather, Shreela, 167
France, 95, 96, 99–101 *passim* 113, 157, 169, 171
Francophone countries, 95–101 *passim*
Francophonie, La, 96, 98–101, 169
Fraser, Malcolm, 31–3, 73, 76, 133, 141, 171, 174
Frisch, Dieter, 157
Front Line States, 64, 74, 85, 90, 93, 142
Froude, James Anthony, 47–8
Fyjis-Walker, Dick, 122

Gairy, Sir Eric, 148, 150
Galt, Sir Alexander, 43
Gambia, The, 154
Gandhi, Indira, 7, 18, 20, 111, 134
  Mahatma, 58, 113
  Rajiv, 7, 62, 64, 70, 81–2, 86, 137, 146, 166, 167, 169
Ganilau, Ratu Sir Penaia, 87
Garba, Brig. Joe, 139
Garner, Joe, 10–13 *passim*
Garvey, Marcus, 11
de Gaulle, General, 9
Gayoom, President, 145, 146, 150
Geest, 157
George V, 111, 113
George VI, 7, 110, 113
Germany, 50, 53, 93, 125, 157
Ghana, 10, 12, 64, 132, 142, 169, 170
Gibbs, Oswald, 148, 156
Globe and Mail (Toronto), 82
Gooch, Graham, 134, 135
Gorbachev, President, 93
Greater Britain, 46
Greathead, Dr, 125
Greece, 157
Grenda, 65, 109, 110, 145–51 *passim*, 154
Grey, Lord, 39
Gunn, Richard, 151, 157
Guyana, 18, 19, 95, 134, 183n3
Gwyn, Richard, 96

Hammarskjold, Dag, 19
Harcourt, Sir William, 45
Hawke, Bob, 8, 31, 64–6 *passim*, 70, 72, 73, 81, 106, 127, 163–4
Hayden, Bill, 107, 123, 127

Heath, Edward, 16, 81, 140
Hertzog, General, 56
Heseltine, Sir William, 123, 127
Hitler, Adolf, 86
Hong Kong, 37, 158
Hospitality for Overseas Students, 128
Howe, Sir Geoffrey, 24, 75–80, 82, 83, 90, 168
Hughes, Cledwyn, 13
Hume, A. O., 51
human rights, 170
Hungary, 125

Imperial
  College, 119, 125
  Federation League, 47
  Institute, 119–21
Imperial Commonwealth, 52
India/Indians, 5–9 *passim*, 18, 35, 36, 43, 45, 51, 53, 56–8 *passim*, 71, 91, 113, 116–17, 134, 135, 137–8, 142, 145–6, 149, 150, 165–70 *passim*, 173, 181n8
Indian Ocean, 93
Indonesia, 102, 163
Industrial Development Unit, 29
Ingham, Bernard, 71, 72, 84, 86
Institute of Commonwealth Studies, Oxford, 126; London, 126–7
International Defence and Aid Fund, 23, 67
International Monetary Fund, 86, 90, 170
Ireland, 56, 96
Irwin, Lord (Lord Halifax), 58
Israel, 93, 101
Italy, 92
Jackman, Robin, 133–4
Jamaica, 95, 153, 155, 157, 183n3
Japan, 102, 125, 154, 161, 163, 165, 181n8, 184n2
Jayewardene, President, 145, 146
Just, H. W., 49, 50

Kaunda, Kenneth, 64, 70, 76, 78–9, 81, 82, 84–6 *passim*, 90, 147
Kenya, 10, 78, 91, 95, 142, 150
Kerr, Philip (Lord Lothian), 52
Kerr, Sir John, 107
Kilgore, Arthur, 30
King, Mackenzie, 161

INDEX

Kiribati, 131, 172
Kitchener, Lord, 48, 53
Kohl, Chancellor, 76
Kruger, Paul, 49

Labour Shows the Way, 58
Landry, Monique, 97
Lange, David, 108–9, 118, 163
language sciences, 99
Lansbury, George, 58
Latin America, 143, 156
League of Nations, 36, 51, 55
Lee Kuan Yew, 173
LePan, Douglas, 96
Lesotho, 76, 92, 132, 142
Limpopo railway line, 93
Lloyd George, David, 55
Lomé Conventions, 94, 95, 157
Luthufi, Abdulla, 145, 146, 150
Lutyens, Sir Edwin, 5, 57
Luxembourg, 99
Luyt, Louis, 143

Macaulay, Thomas B., 35, 36
Machel, President, 23, 76, 79
Mackenzie, William Lyon, 39
Macmillan, Harold, 11, 60, 70
Makatini, Johnstone, 70
Malan, D. F., 54, 110
Malawi, 10, 91, 93, 95, 142
Malaysia, 169, 173
Maldives, 145–6, 149, 150, 154, 172
Malecela, John, 73
Mancham, President James, 149–50
Mandela, Nelson, 71, 74, 76, 77, 94, 133; Winnie, 76
Manley, Norman, 155
Margaret, Princess, 129
Marlborough House, 26, 112
Marshall, Sir Peter, 129
Martinique, 157
Mauritius, 95
Maxwell, Robert, 142
Mayall, James, 35
Mbeki, Thabo, 143
McWilliam, Michael, 128–9
Melbourne, Lord, 39–41 *passim*
membership, Commonwealth, 169, 185
Menzies, Robert, 7–9 *passim*, 11, 32, 55
  Foundation, 127

Mexico, 102
Mill, James, 35; John Stuart, 35, 38
Millar, Tom, 127, 162, 164
Miller, J. F. B., 17
Milner, Sir Alfred, 48–52 *passim*, 54, 76
mini-states, 11, 145–58, 171–2
Minorco, 87
Mitterrand, President, 99, 100
Mission to South Africa: The Commonwealth Report, 75
Mizoram, 132
Modern Commonwealth, The, 9
Mohamad, Dr Mahathir, 173
Molesworth, Sir William, 37
monarchy, 8–9, 57, 80, 104–18, 148, 149 *see also individual headings*
Monarchy to Republic, 106
Monde, Le, 100
Montgomery, Bill, 29
Morley-Minto reforms, 51
Morocco, 99
Mozambique, 29, 76, 83, 91–4 *passim*, 101
Mugabe, Robert, 21, 64, 65, 76, 81, 85, 86, 141, 147
Muldoon, Sir Robert, 20, 139–41 *passim*
Mulroney, Brian, 32, 64, 65, 70, 80–2, 85–7 *passim*, 101, 104, 161, 172
Murdoch, Rupert, 161
Mururoa atoll, 154

Nacala railway line, 93
Nagaland, 132
Namibia, 29, 67, 78, 83, 93, 94, 169
Naoroji, Dadabhai, 51
Nassau Fellowship Fund, 29
National Congress, Indian, 51, 57, 58
Nauru, 131
Négritude, 100, 101
Nehru, Motilal, 7; Pandit, 7, 113
New Commonwealth, 7–10 *passim*, 28, 30, 165–7, 173 *see also individual countries*
New International Economic Order, 28, 62, 170
New Zealand, 1, 2, 6, 44, 51, 54–6 *passim*, 106, 139, 140, 143, 149, 159, 163, 164

Newcastle, Duke of, 114
Newfoundland, 51
Nigeria, 10, 16, 68–70 *passim*, 74, 78, 132, 139, 142, 169, 170
Njonjo, Charles, 101
Nkomo, Joshua, 21
Nkrumah, Kwame, 3, 10–12 *passim*, 100–1
Non-Aligned Movement, 64, 85
non-governmental organizations (NGOs), 129–30, 174
North Atlantic Treaty Organization, 56
North-South Institute, 80
North-South relations, 111, 141, 171
Nyerere, Julius, 3, 31, 97, 139

Obasanjo, Gen. Olusegun, 73, 74
Obote, Milton, 170
oil, 69, 157
Okanagan Statement on Southern Africa, 62, 87
Old Commonwealth, 6, 20, 26, 27, 109, 123, 149, 159–65, 173 *see also individual countries*
Olympia and York, 160
Olympic Games, 136, 137, 139
Organization African Unity, 64, 85
Organization for Economic Co-operation and Development, 91, 92
Overseas Development Administration, 102, 127

Pacific, 94, 153–4, 163, 164
 South – Bureau for Economic Co-operation, 154
 South – Forum, 154
Pakistan, 56, 166, 169, 170
Palliser, Sir Michael, 65
Palmer, Geoffrey, 172
Palmerston, Lord, 39
'pan-Anglicanism', 46–7
Papineau, Louis-Joseph, 39, 41
Papua New Guinea, 62, 153, 154
49th Paradox, The, 96
Patten, Christopher, 94–5, 102
peacekeeping force, 150–1
Pearson, Lester, 12, 96, 98
Philip, Prince, 15, 106, 108
Pindling, Sir Lynden, 66–7, 152
Pitcairn Island, 115

population growth, 90
Porter, James, 122
Portugal, 101, 157
poverty, 170
preferences, imperial, 55, 94, 161
Prince Edward Island, 131
Princess Royal, 108
Royal of the Commonwealth, The, 52
Punjab, 132, 166

Quebec, 98, 105–6, 161
Queen Mother, 104, 129

Rabuka; Colonel, 149
racism, 3, 10, 42, 47, 49, 50, 51, 53, 64, 89, 140, 155, 167
Radical Imperialists, 35, 46
Ramphal, Shridath, 5, 18–33 *passim* 67, 69, 72, 75, 85, 112, 140, 141, 146, 150, 170, 172
Ramsamy, Sam, 134, 144
Reading, Lord, 57
Reform Act (1832), 35, 39
Register of Sports with South Africa, 134
Reid, Stuart, 39
Renamo, 93, 94
René, Albert, 62, 149–50
Renouf, Alan, 32
Reichmann brothers, 159–60, 162
Rhodes, Cecil, 40, 53, 126
 House, 126
Rhodesia, 12, 15, 16, 21–2, 64, 70, 77, 79, 100, 139, 170
Robinson, Bobby, 136
Roebuck, John Arthur, 38
Rose, Sir John, 115
Rosebery, Lord, 36, 45
Round Table, The, 52, 54
Royal Commonwealth Society, 23, 74, 94, 127–30
Royal Empire Society, 53, 128
Royal family, 7, 108–15, 129
rugby, 20, 133, 139, 140, 142–4 *passim*, 164
 Gondwanaland – Federation, 143
rum, 95
Russia, 50
Rwanda, 99

Salim, Salim, 31

sanctions, 2, 16, 22, 31, 64–72, 75–7, 80–2, 84–9 passim, 112, 136, 142, 143, 166, 169
Sanders, Ron, 151–3 passim 155, 156
SAN–ROC, 134
Sandys, Duncan, 9, 12
Saunders, Norman, 153
Sauvé, Governor-General jeanne, 104, 105
science, 99, 100
Scoon, Sir Paul, 148–50 passim
Scott, Archbishop Edward, 73
Secretariat, Commonwealth, 5, 9, 10, 12–33, 69, 95, 100, 112, 124, 130, 145, 150, 154, 168, 172, 174
   Agreed Memorandum (1963), 10, 13–14, 26, 69, 112
   finance, 25–30
Secretary-General, 2, 13–15, 18, 30–3, 62, 146, 174
Seeley, John, 47
Senegal, 100
Senghor, President, 100–1
Seychelles, 62, 149–50, 154
Sharp, Mitchell, 97
Sierra Leone, 1, 10
Singapore, 173
Singh, Sardar Swaran, 73
Smith, Arnold, 15–16, 18, 21, 27
Smith, Ian, 16, 21–2, 77
Smuts, Jan, 53–4, 56, 110
Solomon Islands, 130, 154
South Africa, 2, 6, 10, 11, 20, 22–3, 29, 31, 47–51, 53–6, 60, 64–89, 90, 92–4, 101, 110, 126, 131, 133–5, 139–44, 163, 166, 169, 170, 175
South Korea, 102
Soviet Union, 19, 93, 168
Spain, 101, 157
sport, 20, 67, 133–44, 164
Springboks, 20, 139–41 passim, 143
Spycatcher case, 107
Sri Lanka, 145, 170, 173
St Lucia, 154
Stanfield, Robert, 106
Stephen, Sir Ninian, 107
Stockmar, Baron, 113, 114
students, 24, 126–8 passim
Sudan, 99
sugar, 95, 157
summits, 23, 61–3, 98, 130, 169

Cancun (1981), 141
Delhi (1983), 65, 147
francophone, 99–100
Kingston (1975), 18
Kuala Lumpur (1989), 2, 87, 169, 172–4 passim
London (1965), 10, 12, 13; (1977), 32, 139; (1986), 2, 24, 64, 80–4, 172
Lusaka (1979), 21–2, 31
Melbourne (1981), 20, 106, 140–1, 149
Nassau (1985), 2, 24, 62, 64–72, 150, 172
regional 32, 154
Singapore (1971), 81, 98, 140, 170
Vancouver (1987), 2, 24, 25, 61, 62, 64, 83–8, 111, 172, 180n7
Sunday Times, The, 80
Swaziland, 76, 95
Switzerland, 99

Taiwan, 93
Tamil Nadu, 132
Tanzania, 3, 10, 26, 53, 64, 91, 93, 95, 97, 142, 149, 150
technical assistance, 28–30 *see also* CFTC
   Group, 29
   TCDC, 30
technology, 99, 100
Testing Time, A, 67
Thailand, 29
Thatcher, Margaret, 2, 7, 8, 21–4, 31–3 passim, 59, 64–6, 69–72, 75–82, 84–6, 88–90 passim, 108, 112, 136, 142, 147, 163, 166, 168, 169, 172
Thomson, Lord, 161
Thorne, Maj.-Gen. Sir David, 129
Tonkin, David, 131–2
trade, 37, 55, 68–9, 71, 86, 87, 90, 94–5, 156–8, 161, 169
transatlantic alliance, 46, 53, 59
Transvaal, 49, 50
treaties
   India-Soviet Union Friendship, 168
   South Pacific Nuclear Free Zone, 154
Vereeniging, 48–50 passim, 53
Versailles, 55

Trent case, 115
Trinidad, 95, 155, 157, 183n3
Trudeau, Pierre, 97–8, 105, 106, 139, 161
Tsang, Joseph, 130
Tunisia, 99
Turks and Caicos Islands, 153
Turner, John, 161
Turton, Thomas, 40
Tutu, Bishop Desmond, 76
Tuvalu, 172

Uganda, 10, 65, 95, 132, 139, 142, 170
unemployment, 156
United Nations, 2, 18–19, 28, 51, 85, 90, 91, 94, 125, 154, 172, 173
  Conference on Trade and Development, 64
  Development Programme, 125
  blacklist, 134
  Committee on Apartheid, 139
  Security Council, 19
  Special Session on Africa, 90
United States, 2, 6, 11, 19, 38, 39, 43, 46, 47, 53, 55, 56, 59, 65, 93, 94, 96–7, 101, 102, 105, 114, 115, 146–8, 151, 152, 154, 161, 162

Venezuela, 102
Victoria, Queen, 5, 43–4, 114–17 *passim*, 119
Victoria League, 128–9

Wakefield, Edward Gibbon, 38, 40
Waldheim, Kurt, 18
war
  Algerian, 100
  American Civil, 115
  Boer, 36, 47–8
  civil, 90
  Vietnam, 100
  World, First, 53; Second, 1, 8, 34, 53, 56
Wavell, Lord, 113
Welensky, Roy, 10
West India Committee, 129
West Indians, 155, 156
West Indies, 133–4
  Federation, 154–5, 183n8
Western Samoa, 154
Westminster, Statute, of, 55
Wheeler-Bennett, John, 110
Whitlam, Gough, 107
Williams, Eric, 155
Wilson, Harold, 13, 16
Windward Islands, 155–8
Wingti, Paias, 62
Winterton, George, 106
withdrawals, from Commonwealth, 11, 80, 89, 98, 110, 168, 170
Wood, Bernard, 80
World Bank, 90, 125, 129, 170
Wright, Sir Patrick, 123

Zaire, 99
Zambia, 10, 64, 68, 71, 76, 79, 89, 91
Zimbabwe, 10, 21, 71, 76, 78, 85, 93, 95, 150

...SON COLLEGE